ARE YOU LIVING LIFE OR IS LIFE LIVING YOU?

Becoming a Victor and Not a Victim

B O B   B O X E R

ISBN: 1479291226
ISBN 13: 9781479291229

ACKNOWLEDGMENTS

It is with great appreciation that I thank the people who made this possible. Their lives, their inspiration have touched my life in ways too numerous to list.

The students of Boys and Girls Republic — Who have taught me more than I have taught them.

The ministries of Dr. Ralph Didier, Rev. Billy Graham, and Bishop T.D. Jakes — Who have given me insight and have shown me what it is to be a man of God.

My family and especially my wife Deborah — Who has loved me through the ups and downs of our somewhat "different" life.

Most of all I thank God — Who has never left me, even when I felt alone. Who has taken what I thought was a curse and turned it into the greatest blessing of my life. To Him be the praise and glory forever!

.

INTRODUCTION

I look around every day, and I see people who, in a sense, just exist, going through the motions of life, *controlled by anger, hurt, and fear.* They let negative thoughts or emotions run their lives and seem to endlessly repeat the same mistakes. Many people lurch from one bad relationship or situation to another, and they don't know why. Maybe this sounds like you. Are you frustrated with your life? Do you want to make a change? The Bible says there is an answer!

> *Yet in all these things [the trials of life], we are more than conquerors through Him who loved us. For I am persuaded that neither death nor life, nor angels nor principalities nor powers nor things present nor things to come. Nor height nor depth nor any created thing shall be able to separate us from the love of God which is in Christ Jesus our Lord.*
> —Romans 8:37–39

Do you know that you are loved? Do you know that no matter what you are facing or whatever you have gone through, God loves you, and in His time, He will use it for His glory? Do you know that your life is not a mistake? *Does what you believe about life give you real hope and peace?* Or are you crying, struggling, and searching for an answer, but God seems silent, and life keeps beating you down? Do you feel like quitting? Paul was chained on the outside, but he was free on the inside. Paul was writing this to Christians who were facing death and persecution.

Do you feel enslaved by your own emotions and circumstances? Today, with all our scientific advances, with all our institutions of higher learning, and with our so-called spirituality, do you still struggle to find happiness? Do you really know God's love? Paul's words are true. These are more than just feel-good words. This is the heart and soul of the Bible.

Maybe you feel that you can never win. Your money is tight; your health fading; your family and your personal relationships are a mess; and the world around you looks as if it is going crazy.

If you believe that Paul's words are true and realize how much God, through Christ, loves you, *you can know victory*; you can know *God's peace* in any situation!

Jesus said, "In this world you will have tribulation, but be of good cheer; I have overcome the world."-John 16:33b

Motivations

Before I go any further, I need to ask some important questions, and how you answer will determine success or failure. Do you really want to change or grow? Do you feel that God might be trying to get your attention? Are life's circumstances convincing you that you need to do something different? Are you like the prodigal son who needs to come home? Is what you are doing working?

All of us have struggles and trials in life. The question is: Will we let our past hurts control us, or will we use them to grow and to help others?

My prayer is that this is not just another self-help book to read. My hope is for something better: I pray that it will be a change in the direction of your life—a new beginning in which you will be helping yourself to live a more satisfying and happy life. My thought is that through changing yourself, you can influence the world around you for the better. If you can think you can change, you are just a new thought away from a new you. Your money is not the problem; your car or your friends or your addictions are not the problem. *Your thoughts and feelings about them are the problems.* No one can do the work for you. For the most part, you must do it for yourself. The questions at the end of each chapter are easy, and they work if you put in the effort and are honest with yourself. Remember this: there is an answer. When you bring your life and your problems to the foot of the cross and truly apprehend God's love, you can find the answer to your individual needs. As long as you are alive, you have the opportunity to change and to grow. Even life's struggles are an opportunity.

Paul tells us: "I can do all things through Christ who strengthens me." Philippians 4:13

The most important tool for change is *honesty*.

It is the secrets that we keep from ourselves and others that control us. Honesty to self and others is foundational. I will be asking you to answer some fundamental—but potentially insightful—questions. My goal is for you to get a better handle on your life and to develop insights to help you understand why you do what you do. From these insights you can develop goals and a plan to truly live life rather than letting life's circumstances control you. Too many of us spend years of our lives controlled by fears or past hurts and anger. We become mired in responses that just don't work. We self-medicate with drugs or food, spend hours escaping through the fantasy of media, and become obsessive over relationships with others and things—all in a fruitless attempt to find joy in the fleeting moments of happiness.

Romans 8:6 states: "The mind set on the flesh [worldly things, emotions, greed, and sensuality] is death [spiritual death, the loss of peace and love, the relationship with God and others], but the mind set on the spirit is life and peace."

The question is: *"Are you going to listen to your emotions or deal with the truth?"*

This is about becoming a *victor* in life rather than a *victim*. It is about gaining that peace. It is about changing your attitude toward yourself and others. It is about changing the way that you think about things. How we think controls our lives.

Proverbs 23:7 states: *"As a man thinks in his heart so he is."*

I have spent the last thirty-plus years counseling others. They have taught me as well. Developing these insights has made me a better and emotionally healthier person. This leads me to the question: Are you living life, or is life living you?

My point is that God wants you to live to enjoy Him and the life that He has given you. Is that not true worship? Is that not real happiness? God has a purpose in your life, and He has called you to get out of the rut—called you to grow and to change. Your life is a blessing.

So what's the problem?

Chapter 1

CHANGE YOUR MIND

Therefore, I urge you, brothers and sisters, in view of God's mercy, to offer your bodies as a living sacrifice holy and pleasing to God—this is true and proper worship. Do not be conformed to the pattern of this world but be transformed by the renewing of your mind. Then you will be able to test and approve what God's will is—His good and pleasing perfect will. —Romans 12:1ff

The first question you need to ask yourself honestly is: *"Are you happy with your life?"* If you are totally happy with who you are and how your life is going, then I would say that you see no need to change or to read this book. Rephrasing the question might prove useful: Is what you are doing working for you? Is this where you want to be in your life? If you were to die tonight, what hopes and dreams would you miss out on? Do you like who you are? Is this what you wanted for yourself? If the answer to any of these questions is no, then the problem becomes finding out why or figuring out what is not working and changing it. The truth is this: *"If you keep doing what you are doing then you will keep getting what you are getting." If you keep thinking the way you think, you will keep reacting the way you do. Do you like what you are getting these days? Do you like who you are?*

There is a way to change your life: it is in changing your mind and how you think about things. It is about being transformed by the power and love of God. From that you can learn God's will and purpose for your life.

I spent years trying to change my life on my own. Truth be told, I was running from life. I started when I was young by running to my room when things were crazy in my home, and as I got older, that progressed to going to my room and smoking a joint. Later, that moved to running away from home and staying high most of the time. This type of escapism and withdrawal led me to the point of suicide, which was the ultimate escape! I thought suicide would work to solve the pain of living. In a strange sense, I was right. A point to remember is that though a person may *display very strange behavior,* to him or her it *makes sense.* In fact, suicide was the logical extension of a behavior that I had practiced for many years. But *one thought* changed my life forever. That thought was "Jesus personally loves me." Within a short period of time, I began to realize that I didn't need drugs; I didn't want that old life. My soul was saved; my heart was changed, but my head was still making readjustments. God wasn't done with His work in me yet.

He is not done with you yet. Real transformation takes time. For the Lord, it is a lifetime process, working in us and through us. That is why you should never judge God by Christians. God is perfect, but we're not; He's not done with us yet.

It is through learning to deal with the *stress of life* that people are transformed. Give a person a tough job—a responsibility—and most of the time he or she will rise to the occasion. That is why entitlement programs don't work: because they teach you to be dependent, and dependence leads to anger. That is why I believe that God tests all believers: to make us learn to trust and love Him. Look at your life; you have been through some tough times, and you are still standing. You are still here. God has been there with you through all of it. He is working His will in your life.

Psalm 66:10: "For you, O God tested us, you refined us like silver."

It is through our struggles that we are molded into who we become, for the better or the worse. It is all about perspective. We don't know how good we have things until they are gone. I am not thankful for my back until it goes out. You are not thankful for the good until you have been through the bad. It is through our struggles that we learn God's will and purpose for our lives. It is how we coped with or perceived adversity in the past that can determine or influence our feelings and choices in the future.

It is also true that through our struggles, we experience God's grace and blessing. It is through the hard times that we learn empathy and the ability to care for others. But there is a choice in how we look at things. We can see the good or obsess on the bad. It is in the hard times that we learn to pray, and it is through difficulties that we learn who we really are. It is through knowledge, time, and perspective that we gain a higher under-standing. You might think that it is evil for a man to cut another man with a knife unless you know that he is a surgeon. God is the great physician and healer.

It might sound strange, but today I have gotten to the point of being able to thank God for the prayers to which He answered no, for the relationships that didn't go as I planned, and for my failures that I thought would never end. Sometimes the things that seemed to be a curse were blessings in disguise. Is it God's will for us to go through the hard times to fulfill His plan for our lives? Remember, whatever you have been through and whatever you are confronted with, God is bigger than your problem. God is in the business of transforming lives, turning trials into testimonies. Isn't that what the cross is all about? God will fulfill a greater purpose in your life if you let Him, or you can let your life and past hurts destroy you. Can you accept where you are at today and move forward with God's help to your new tomorrow? Or will you continue to make the same mistakes over and over again?

In time, I came to realize this important truth: *the only person I can change is me.* In fact, prayer changes me and my thoughts rather than changing God. The only mind I really can change is my own. I need to be responsible for my choices, my actions, and my thoughts. I need to be honest with myself, with others, and with God.

Many of our feelings about life and people are just poor reflections of our past. Many feelings aren't based in reason or truth. They are childish defense mechanisms that we use to protect ourselves. The problem is they invade our present and affect our lives today and how we cope. Do your feelings and negative thoughts control you? I have seen many people living their lives controlled by self lies, negative thoughts, and emotions; they are ruled by fear, expecting the worst to happen. Could it be that the effects of child abuse are related to post-traumatic stress disorder? But our feelings are not the problem; our past is not the problem. It's our thinking and how we interpret our past that controls us.

It is your choice to let the past control you. When you know the God who really loves you, then you don't need acceptance from everyone else. Then you don't need to change the world and everyone around you. You don't focus on your losses and let bitterness run your life. Jesus didn't die on the cross so you could have a miserable life. It is your choice.

Isn't it time to break the chain? Isn't it time to stop the craziness? Isn't it time to live the life that God wants for you? Isn't it time for a new thought, a new understanding, and a new life? Everything starts with your thoughts. The truth is that I am a better counselor because of all the things I have been through. My hurt has given me empathy. Your life is not some mistake, so don't give up. I am not saying that life is fair, and that you might not have real reasons for feeling unhappy, but *self-pity is a wasted emotion.* Real growth happens when we take stock of who we are and where we are at.

Jesus said, "Come unto me and I will give you rest; I will give you peace." In spite of all of our past mistakes, God loves us. Jesus can heal the past hurts; the old is passed away, and He makes all things new. He can and will transform your mind. He has given you the ability to deal with your life where you are right now. You might be waiting on God, but God is waiting on you to submit your mind, your life, your will to Him. That one thought can transform your life.

My point is this: if your life isn't working out so well, if you're controlled by negative thoughts and emotions, if you are stuck on that roller coaster, then maybe it is time to surrender. Maybe you need Christ. He says in the text of the book of Romans to give your body as a living sacrifice.

You might say that you believe in God, but the ultimate question is: Do you know Him? Is He your hope? Is He the first thing you think of in the morning and your last thought at night? Is His presence in your life? Are your prayers answered? Or is church some traditional thing that you "should" do? The Bible says that God loves you—really loves you. Do you know how much? Have you experienced the reality of His love? He wants to bless you.

Dear friends, the battles we face today are over the territories of our minds and our thoughts. We are bombarded by all sorts of negative influences from the world around us.

We have a media that sells its products through greed, want, and sex. The moral world that we face is a "mind" field of wanton permissiveness. Where does it come from?

The Adversary

Dear friend, if God is real, then Satan is real. Satan knows that God loves you, and he hates what God loves. In fact, Satan doesn't understand real love or faith in God. He will attack you in the areas that you care about the most. He knows you and your weaknesses. On the other hand, God knows and loves you. He has given you the ability to stand up with His help to whatever Satan throws your way. God knows what you are going through, and He will help you get through it. Remember: *"the battle belongs to the Lord"* and *"greater is He that is within you, than he that is in the world."*

The Bible says this in Ephesians 6:11ff: *"Therefore [since we live in this fallen and unfair world] put on the whole armor of God that you may be able to stand against the wiles of the devil, for we do not wrestle against flesh and blood but against principalities against powers against the darkness of this age against spiritual hosts of wickedness in the heavenly places...."*

Dear friends, the word *wiles*, *"methodia"* in the original Greek, means mind games, schemes, and trickery. The place the enemy will attack you is in your mind. Remember, he is the father of lies! When someone messes with your mind, he or she messes with your most precious resource. That is why recreational drug use destroys lives.

I have seen his lies; I have even fallen for some. What about you?

There was a time that I didn't want to know how much I weighed. I spent years knowing that things didn't fit right, but getting on the scale was out of the question. I could still squeeze into those size 38 jeans. We tend to believe that what we don't know won't hurt us. How many people avoid going to the doctor? I have heard people say that they weren't sick until they went for the checkup. More commonly, I have heard the statement: "Before I went in for counseling, I didn't have any *real* problems."

People would rather believe a lie, their own fantasies, or false hopes than deal with truth.

It wasn't until the doctor said, "You are obese, and you have diabetes" that I decided to make a change. I lost sixty pounds and started a healthier lifestyle.

I have counseled people who have believed the enemy's lies. They have just given up on life and hope, too afraid to try because they believed they would *always* fail. I have heard this line of thinking from young people with no hope for the future. For the most part, they have been abandoned by parents whose lives center on drugs and self-delusion. They have seen friends killed by drugs or gangs and figure it is just a matter of time until they get shot or go to prison. So it becomes, "Eat, drink, and be merry for tomorrow we die."

This lie of *hopelessness* is from the pit of hell. If your next high, your next binge, your next purchase, your relationship, etc. is all you hope for, you're already as good as dead. It's one of the enemy's oldest tricks. Hopelessness is the lie that says that God doesn't love you. It is the same lie that Satan told Adam and Eve: God is unfair; therefore, life is unfair! God becomes some sort of cosmic policeman who doesn't want you to be happy. This is a lie that pollutes your mind. God really loves you and wants the best for you. God wants you to enjoy Him and the life that He has given you. God placed Adam and Eve in a garden and gave them everything. The truth is that if you can think, if you can look at things in a different way, you can change. You can make your life better. You can evolve. You can take a step up in your life. You can turn your negatives into positives, and your struggles can become opportunities. I am not just talking about some type of positive or new age hype. I am talking about faith and hope in Christ and His power to transform and renew your mind.

Victimization (Blame)

There have been times in my life that I have struggled with depression, drug abuse, obesity, codependence, low self-esteem, etc. The bottom line, in simple terms, is that I was out of control, and I was not happy. Maybe you can relate to some of these things. It doesn't matter what your particular issues are, the question is: What will you do about them? All I knew was that I wasn't happy. I used to blame others, the world, the system, my parents—whatever or whoever was convenient. Some people even blame God when things are hard. Blame is a way to run from responsibility. It will poison your mind and your ability to succeed. Blame is a natural human response. From the beginning of time, even Adam denied responsibility and blamed Eve and God.

Genesis 3:12–13: "The man said, 'The woman whom You gave to be with me, she gave me from the tree, and I ate.'"

How do you feel—too tired or afraid to try, believing that no matter what you do, you cannot win? Many would call this being a victim, blaming the world for your life. This is a self-justifying lie that we tell ourselves. If you see yourself as a victim or that you can never win, you can justify the worst behavior. In your mind, you're already seeing yourself as a loser, so why try? Is that the type of thinking in the mind of suicide bombers? Everything is _____'s fault. I can't win, so I might as well take them with me.

In fact, by *blaming* everyone else, you will never have to take responsibility, and you might even feel good about lashing out at others. I have seen some people, when they are retelling something they have done foolishly (which most of us would see as wrong) smile with some strange sense of satisfaction. Are they saying to God or life, "I will show you, I will hurt you"? If you blame life (your family, the government, etc.), you might as well destroy it, but you will destroy yourself in the process. What kind of logic is that? The truth is that if we blame life, we blame God! Is that why so many turn from faith—because they are angry at life? This type of thinking comes from the pit of hell, and it's a lie. Satan uses it to turn hearts from God. Don't listen to blame.

"Therefore submit yourselves to God. Resist the devil and he will flee from you" *(James 4:7).* Satan wants you to blame God; he wants you to blame life.

One young man in a counseling group told me that his mother died when he was young. I asked him, "So you hate God, right?"

He replied with glee, "Yes, and that's why I'm an atheist."

I asked, "How can you be angry at someone whom you say you don't believe exists?"

Are you angry at God?

Maybe it is more like how people rationalize not trying, not believing, because in their mind it is better to not try—not have faith and fail—rather than to try and fail. At least you have some control. Then you can then say to yourself, "I really didn't care."

But this too is a lie of the devil. The truth is that everyone has failures, but those who quit trying in life are the ones who really lose.

It wasn't until I stopped running, stopped blaming, and started confronting my life that things began to change.

Denial

Now you might be saying to yourself, "This isn't for me. I don't want to be religious; I don't need that." You're right. What I am talking about is a relationship with the almighty God. If the God of the Bible is real, that would mean that I would need to make some changes in the way that I think, act, and feel about life. *Is it easier to believe a lie or to deal with the truth?* Most of us would rather believe a lie because it is too hard to deal with the truth. Your lifestyle and what you do seem normal to you. It is what you know, and it makes you happy—or does it?

There are reasons and real reasons!

Have you ever seen the TV show *American Idol*? Have you noticed that in the first rounds of the singing contest there are some pretty bad singers? The funny thing is that they think they can sing. Maybe people are afraid to tell them the truth. The sad thing is that the stranger they are, the worse they sing, and the more they *need* to believe the lie that they are going to be a star. In a sense, it is easier to believe the lie than to deal with the reality of their life. The more desperate their need, the greater the anger they show to the judges who tell them the truth. They don't want to hear the truth! Their fantasy (our addictions, our bigotries, our vices) have become normal. It is not until the reality of life becomes so hard (like the prodigal son) that we are willing to change. We don't want to look at the truth of our lives. I wonder if down inside, they really know the truth. I have been told that a good therapist tells people what they really already know down inside but will not admit to themselves.

For years my feelings of abandonment and the consequences of how I dealt with them were a major part of my life, even if I didn't see them. I did all sorts of things to cope with the depression, the anger, and the feelings of rejection that accompanied issues with my father. Sometimes I think that our issues push us to the careers or jobs we seek. I want to be heard, so I become a public speaker or teacher or counselor. Does what we weren't or what we wanted growing up *(our need)* draw us to who we become?

Symptoms versus the real issue

You might ask, "What do I mean by all of this?" What I am trying to say is that our issues—like drug use, anger, sexual addiction, etc.—are symptoms of other problems. You might have an explosive temper, but underneath, it could be feelings of *hurt, fear, or frustration.* The real issue of my life is *withdrawal—running away.* That is how I dealt with my family—especially my father—growing up.

You see, for example, the problem isn't drugs. The problem is me and my messed-up mind—the way I look at things and cope. You might call it immaturity, selfishness, or a disease—whatever—but God calls it sin. A drug used correctly saves lives and is really a gift from God. The real question you should be asking yourself is: Why is it that the only way I seem to have fun or enjoy my life is when I am stoned or eating, shopping, or whatever your issue or obsession is? Why do you need this thing so much? What problem or pain are you self-medicating? What really hurts? You must come to the realization that you are being controlled by your *need.* Why do you *need* to do brain damage, physical injury, or financial harm to enjoy life? The truth is that God is the only one that can meet the needs of your life and bring true lasting happiness.

So I ask: What is the real problem, issue, or hurt in your life? What or who hurt you the most growing up? What was your greatest struggle? Does it color the way you look at life?

God can and will heal those memories if you seek Him. He can use your pain for His glory to help others, or you can let it control you. Remember: God took mankind's cruelest act, *"the cross,"* and used to save us. That's why it is called Good Friday. God is in the business of turning evil into good, all to His glory. You can let life make you a bitter angry person, or you can use it to make the world a better place. It is your choice.

Aren't you tired of wasting years of your life without real peace? The text says to be renewed, be transformed within your mind. It is a choice to take on the new and let go of the old way of thinking. It is a choice to trust the Lord and believe; your life is not some accident. You are not a victim of life. In Christ there is freedom, power, and joy. Jesus said, "I came that you might have life more abundantly." But you need to change your mind and let go of the past hurts and jealousies, hate, and old perspectives. Be made new and let Christ come in. Don't do things in the old way. Learn to be thankful for the life that you have been given. It is a choice to trust and to rejoice in the Lord always.

So I ask you this question: Are you in control of your life, or is life (drug use, anger, impulsiveness, overeating, etc.) controlling you? Again, are you really happy?

God loves you. Now is the time to get rid of the distractions and the negative thoughts that get in the way of your new life. It is time to break the chain that ties you to your yesterdays. It is time to not let the past control your tomorrow. Look where you are at and see what God has promised you. "God so loved the world [you] that He gave His only begotten son that whosoever believes [trusts] in Him will not perish but have eternal life" (Jn. 3:16). That new life is now. It is time to get some peace and direction in your life. It is time for one new great thought. It is your thoughts that will bring you up or bring you down.

There is hope! It starts by answering the question: *What do I really want for my life?*

I remember a funeral some years ago. The deceased was the father of a friend. He had been remarried, and his ex-wife and children were there. He basically abandoned them. All I saw on their faces were anger, bitterness, and disgust. It was as though they were saying, "I am glad you are dead." It was at that moment that I had a great thought. I made it a goal in my life to really make my family a priority. The question to me was: What do you want them to say or feel about you at your funeral? I want them to love and respect who I was and what I stood for. If I can't accomplish this, what's the point?

My question to you is: *What on earth do you really want, and what do you want to be remembered for?* Personally, at the end of my life, I want to hear the words, *"Well done, thou good and faithful servant."*

The Bible teaches us that God speaks to us through the power of the Holy Spirit. I pray that He is doing that today. God can give us a new mind and a new way of looking at life, but we must give our hearts completely to Him. It is through Christ that we are given a new nature, a new thought life, and peace through the storm. His perfect love casts out fear: the fear of life and the fear of change.

Has Christ changed you and given you a new way of thinking? Yes, you still have problems; you still have loss; but now you have peace and joy in the midst of them.

Has Christ given you a new heart and a new mind? Are you sure of it? Are there still areas where Christ needs to work in you? You can be standing at the grave of a loved one with tears in your eyes, but your heart can rejoice.

Even in hard times, Paul could sing praise to the Lord. He went on to say in Romans chapter 8, *"In all these things we are more than conquerors through Christ who loved us."* He knew that God was in control: *"That all things work together for the good for those who love God and are called according to His purpose."* Do you know His purpose for you? Could you trust God like that? Do you have that hope, that peace, that faith?

Let Jesus renew your mind. Let Him come into your heart. He can do it right now! It takes making that choice to face yourself and the truth of who you are and giving yourself to Christ. No matter what you have done, He can forgive you through the power of the cross. He can make it right. I don't know how He does it. I only know it happens. I know that He died for you—to heal your broken life. His life was broken so that you might be healed. Let Him change you today. The Bible says that God loves you so much that He gave His only begotten Son so that if you believe and trust in Him, you will have eternal life. That life is *now*!

Chapter 1   **Self Questions**

1. Are you happy? Is this where you want to be in your life? Do you like who you are? Who are you really? Is this what you wanted for yourself?

2. What do you really want out of life? What do feel you need most? Will that make you happy? What is your passion? What do you care about?

3. Is what you are doing getting you what you want? What is it getting you?

4. "If you keep doing what you are doing, you will keep getting what you are getting." What does that mean? What will you keep getting? If you continue to think and act the way you do, where will you be in ten years?

5. Do you feel you have a problem? Why or why not? What does it mean to you? "It is easier to believe a lie than deal with the truth." What lies have you believed? What did it cost you?

6. How do you feel about this statement: *"Our addictions, our fears, our losing of our temper, our negative attitudes and feelings, etc. are symptoms of our real issues"? In fact, our feelings about life are a reflection of our past.* What is the biggest issue in your life today? What or with who was your greatest struggle growing up? Does it affect you today? How might your issues today relate to the pain, hurt, or struggles of your past? Does it effect your choices and therefore your future?

7. How did you cope with pain or stress in the past? Did it work? What were your thoughts about it? From today's point of view, were those thoughts logical? How do you deal with stress today? Is it similar what you did in the past? What is God's point of view?

8. What is your greatest fear? What do you do or where do you go to feel safe or secure? How might it control your life today?

9. What has your issue (hurt, anger, depression, etc.) cost you? What have you lost in your life because of the way you think about or cope (anger, drug use, overeating, etc.) with life?

10. Do you want to change? Why or why not? If you change your attitude or the way you think about things, you can change your actions and life. What attitude or thinking must you change? What motivates you?

11. When will you choose to make a change? Ask someone to hold you to your word.

12. Where do you think your hurt and frustration come from? Does it affect you today? Are your feelings logical?

Personal Example

If I were to answer this issue honestly, I guess I would have to say that the greatest issue for me was my relationship or lack of relationship with my father. In many ways my father was what we today would call abusive. To say the least, I hated him. I was afraid of him or afraid to make a mistake. I could not please him because he was a perfectionist with an unpredictable mean streak. This made knowing what was normal difficult. He had his own issues. The truth is that he wasn't *always* that bad. How this played out for me was that as I grew older, I did not trust or respect anyone who was in authority over me. I thought that I was stupid since it seemed that nothing I did could please my father. So I ran away from hard situations; I manipulated to get things. I was passive aggressive; I expected to fail. It seems that even these days when things are going well, in the back of my mind I think, *Something bad is going to happen.* That is just an old negative thought running through my head.

The difference is that *I realize these are only negative thoughts, and that they are not true.* I don't have to be like that frightened child! Everybody has negative or unreal thoughts at times, but it doesn't make them true. They don't have to control you. It is your choice. Sure, we all get tempted. Sometimes those first thoughts in my head are wrong, but if I am thinking, *If I go there, if I do that, I am in trouble,* then I go for the second thought and think about what is important to me. What do I really want, and will my first thought get me there?

Chapter 1   Homework

YOUR LIFE STORY

This is an important step for healing.

Write your life story from beginning to the present. If it is easier, record it and then listen to it.

Remember: many of our feelings about life are not logical but are reflections of our past.

As you review and think about your life, ask yourself these questions:

- Is there someone who hurt or frustrated you the most growing up? Does it affect you today? Like an annoying song on the radio that you can't get out of your head, can you still hear his or her voice?
- Is there a traumatic event in your past after which your life seemed to change? (An example would be you began feeling depressed, angry, or started to drink or use drugs, etc.)
- Is there someone in your past that made you feel loved? What would he or she say to you today?
- Is there a pattern to the way you deal with problems—like anger or withdrawal? When did it begin?

What are the issues that trigger strong emotions in your life? Have you ever confronted those issues or the people that helped to cause the issue? Sometimes it is good to name names or write letters to those whom you feel have hurt you in the past. You don't even have to send the letter; you might just want to burn it. You need to learn to accept that these people were doing the best they knew how—right or wrong. They had their own issues; maybe they couldn't give you what you needed because they didn't have it to give. Or maybe it is just realizing that, yes, you made mistakes, but some of that garbage wasn't your fault. It is also realizing that whatever happened to you doesn't give you the excuse to quit or fail or hate the world around you or not trust anyone. The real trick in life is realizing who really cares and has your back and who doesn't!

Write a letter to the persons who influenced your life the most. Even if the person has passed away, it is a good exercise. If you wish, you can send them the letter, or you can burn it. Another option is to keep it and read it to yourself when your life seems out of control to help you realize where your frustrations originate. Another way to do this exercise would be to place a chair in front of you and pretend that the "person" is sitting in it and tell him or her how you feel.

Chapter 2
WHAT'S YOUR PATTERN OF LIVING?

Proverbs 16:25 states: "There is a way that seems right to a man but in the end it leads to death."

I have to admit that I have been blessed in my life to be able to travel to all parts of the world, to experience all sort of cultures, and to meet many wonderful and interesting people. I would not call myself a missionary in the traditional sense, but of all the cultures that I have been exposed to, I have come to understand and appreciate "street culture." I have met young people that live in Long Beach, California, but they have never seen the ocean. I have met young people who have seen no options for their future. They sell drugs to put food on the table for their little brothers and sisters. Too often they only know the few miles around the street or the gang area where they live.

Most people are influenced by the background they have grown up in. Culture and environment are powerful things. It is the reason we have a Southern Baptist Church. They became "Southern" to justify the culture of slavery prior to the civil war. Their culture overrode their faith. My wife uses the analogy of meat loaf. She states that the meat loaf (or whatever your favorite food was) that your mother made you growing up is the standard you use to judge all meat loaf. To you, it's the best. It is the same with culture and your background, by which you judge others. For many of us, the family that we grew up in is our standard of normal, even if it was far from it.

Through my thirty-plus years of counseling, I have seen all sorts of people and have heard all kinds of stories. But one thing I have come to believe is that no matter how crazy a behavior seems to be to me, to the person doing it, it makes sense. My point is that people are doing the best they know how to do in order to cope. Too often they just don't see the truth of what they are doing because of their own cultural or need-based bias.

I counseled a young girl whose mother, in a sense, pimped her to her boyfriend so that the family wouldn't be kicked out on the street. Unfortunately, to the mother it made sense. And I remember a teenage girl who told me how great it was to be a prostitute and make easy money, but in the same breath told her roommates how important it was to pray over her food before dinner. This type of thinking was somewhat acceptable from the street culture she grew up in.

The point of this chapter is that we are where we came from. It is from the families or environments we were raised in that we learned to cope with life.

I believe that's why the enemy wants to destroy families. Because it is in families that we learn to deal with and understand life. It is in families that we learn to make our way in the world.

Many of us develop patterns of behavior that we learn from the families and cultures that we grow up in: whether we become a bully and learn to intimidate to get our way or learn to manipulate, play the victim, or whatever we use to get what we want or cope. The problem is that we learn these styles of coping through the eyes and mind of a child. Through the years, I have spent many hours with troubled youth, mostly young men. The one thing that all of them generally have in common is that they don't have a healthy relationship with their fathers. Most have fathers who are absent or who are not involved with their lives. Some have never met their dads. Instead, mom fails at setting boundaries with them, and instead of dads, they are dealing with Mom's multiple boyfriends or with stepdads. Many times when dad is gone, the family is destroyed or dysfunctional.

The Bible says in 1 Corinthians 13:11, *"When I was a child I used to speak as a child, think as a child, reason as child; when I became a man I put away childish things."*

Many people, even though they are adults, still think and act like wounded, immature children. It seems that the old tapes and the old reasoning still apply. If we continue in our childish thinking, we will never be able to show the love and faith that God calls us to. If we are stuck in childish misconceptions, we have a hard time dealing with or attaching to the societies we live in. It is no wonder that these needs lead so many young people to associate with negative peer groups such as gangs.

I was once sitting in a group where a young girl shared that she had been given to her grandmother to live with her. Her mother, a prostitute, thought that it would be a better life for her there. It seems that Grandma was a very "religious" person, and the first night, as the young girl sat at dinner, Grandma asked her to pray over the food. She did as she was asked and finished her prayer with "amen." Suddenly, the grandmother hit her repeatedly. The startled six-year-old asked why. The grandmother stated that she didn't say "in Jesus's name" at the end of her prayer. Now to you or to me, this all sounds crazy. But to the six-year-old, who was now seventeen as she related the story, she still thought that she had done something horrible. I asked her if there was anything a six-year-old could have done to deserve a beating. She said no! It seemed that the light went on in her head. It really wasn't her fault! The problem was that through the years she'd spent a good deal of her life being manipulated and used by others, thinking of herself as not a very good person, and feeling like a victim. The way she dealt with this negative self-label was through delinquency, drug use, prostitution, and her own manipulation of others. This also didn't help her view of God and religion. Sadly, her conclusions made sense in a sick way, but they didn't work. It just led to her self-destructive behavior.

All this being said, we need to look at the way we learn to deal or cope with life and ask ourselves: Is it working? *Is there a pattern?*

Galatians 5:19 warns of the pattern of the works of the flesh: immorality, impurity, sorcery (possibly meaning drug use), hatred, contentions, jealousies, outburst of wrath, selfish ambitions.

In contrast to this, the Bible calls us to walk in the Spirit and to live with an attitude of love, joy, peace, patience, kindness, goodness, and self-control. Paul tells us in Philippians to walk according to the "pattern you have seen in us." He goes on to say, *"Whatever is true, whatever is honorable, whatever is right, whatever is pure, whatever is lovely, anything worthy of praise, let your mind dwell on these things…and the peace of God shall be with you."*

As I have said, the pattern in my life was withdrawal. When I was young, my parents spent a lot of time arguing or, as they would say, "discussing." At first I remember trying as a child to get my opinion heard. I was quickly told to shut up. I have to admit that it isn't that strange that I am drawn to professions where people have to listen to me. Of all the things that hurt me to this day, it is being ignored. The way I dealt with rejection as I grew older was to go to my room, shut the door, and listen to music. As time went by, I would run to my room and get high. Soon I found myself running away from home. Can you see the pattern? Whenever I was hurt, I tried to run. Whether I escaped to my room or through drugs or music, the idea was to get away—to not feel the hurt of being rejected.

The question is this: Do you know who you are? Are you struggling to be the person that your family needs you to be, that your job wants, that your parents want, that your spouse wants, and that God wants?

What do you do when life happens—when you lose your job or there are deadlines at work or your health declines? When the crisis comes, do you run and hide in your bitterness, anger, frustration, or depression? The enemy wants to destroy you and separate you from your family, your friends, and your faith. He wants to rob you of your hope.

Are you just going through the motions in your life and at work or at church? Is there a smile on your face, but underneath you are struggling, angry, hurt, or frustrated? People ask how you are doing, and you say fine, but the truth is that you feel ready to explode or give up. I sit in groups with young men who have multiple problems in their lives, but they insist that there is nothing wrong. But that frustration comes out in destructive ways like drinking or drug use, pornography, violence, and gang involvement.

Is there a pattern to the way you deal with stressful issues or drama in your life?

If you are having a hard time answering this question let me pose it like this: If you just found out that someone close to you (like a mother or brother) had died or had been killed, what would your first response be? Would you get angry or think about self-medicating with alcohol or drugs? Would you just not believe it or try to ignore it? Would you think why me, or that this wasn't fair? Maybe you would just work harder and try to control everything.

I remember when my mother had her stroke, which eventually killed her. As I was driving home from the hospital, I was thinking about getting high. Now, I had not used drugs for over ten years, but this negative response was still in my head. Then I reasoned with myself how stupid that would be and remembered all the responsibilities that I had and even my reputation. So I didn't use. I just wanted to run away and not feel the pain. It was that pattern that I had learned through the years. Old habits are hard to change. Some fifteen years later, while watching the twin towers fall, I remember that my first response was to go the refrigerator and self-medicate with food. Maybe this response was not as dramatic, but the idea was still the same: get away, change my consciousness, medicate, and comfort myself with food.

In the past, how have you coped when bad things happened? Is there a pattern? Is how you are coping working? Did it hurt you in the long run? Would others think you were acting crazy? Where did you learn to react the way that you do?

I learned to withdraw within the family that I grew up in. It was how I coped with the drama. It also affected the way I look at others and the expectations that I have for others.

What have you done to get your needs met or to try to cope?

From your childhood, what are your expectations for yourself and others? What are your expectations of life? What are our expectations for God? Remember, for many of us, our representation of God growing up was our parents.

Some Typical Negative Patterns and Coping Styles

1. Withdrawal

As I have said, this is the way I tend to cope, at least it's how I coped in the past. It is the desire to run away, deny the problem, and self-medicate. I look at all drug use as withdrawal and escapism. Underneath there is a fear to face whatever the issue may be. This is a preferred method for many people. It is not that escaping is always wrong, but if you are a one-trick pony you can get yourself into trouble. My question to myself and others is: What are you escaping from, and when did it start? What happened?

2. Passive-aggressive thoughts or behavior

This is somewhat related to withdrawal. It is where, at least in your mind, it is not safe to share how you really feel, so you hold things inside. You don't openly let your feelings or thoughts be known, but those thoughts might come out in the form of sarcastic comments under your breath or by ignoring the problem. This thinking shows itself by telling people what they want to hear and disregarding their requests of you. The truth is that you might be angry, but you were either taught not to show it or you are afraid to show it. Like the person who will not return your call or your text, but they smile to your face. It can be the husband who comes home from work and wants to be left alone, but his wife asks him to take out the garbage, and he says yes but "forgets to do it." This type of person can be very frustrating. In reality, he or she has a hard time facing others and himself or herself.

3. Intimidation

Many people use this style to force others to give them what they want. In the extreme, they really don't care about anyone but themselves. These types might run companies or end up in prison. Everything is about their wants and needs. Underneath, many times, are feelings of fear and weakness. They were hurt growing up, so now they will do the hurting. They were controlled, so now they will do the controlling. These are people who bully with their words or their actions to get what they want. They prey on other people's insecurities and fears. This really is not about being strong or assertive. It is about striking at others in weakness. Not everyone like this becomes a sociopath, but they lean that way. They might not break the law because they don't want to hurt themselves. The truth is that they really don't care about you or know how to care; in fact, they might even get some pleasure in hurting you because it makes them feel better about themselves. In working with gang members, I have seen this over and over again: when a young man gets a disappointing phone call and ends up starting a fight with the first person who walks by. It is best to stay out of an intimidator's way because he or she leaves paths of destruction in his or her life and in the lives of others.

4. Manipulation

Like the child who learns at a young age that if he or she cries long enough he or she will get his or her way or attention. This person is the ultimate game player. Manipulators know, if not instinctively, how to get others to do what they want. They might have grown up feeling "less than" others, so they work harder to get their way. They have the hardest time hearing the word *no*. In their need, they wear others down until they get what they want. They can bug you to death to get their needs met. This can be very frustrating because they don't give up until they get their way, whether right or wrong. They can make great salespeople or maybe even politicians.

5. Impulsive

This is the type of individual who acts without thinking—a person, who, if there is a perceived opportunity jumps at it without thinking about the consequences. Their motto is "if it feels good do it." If someone says, "Let's go to Vegas," they drop what they are doing, and they are there. These people, in a childlike fashion, know how to have fun. But for the most part, they have people picking up the pieces after their adventures. Too many parents, to their own dismay, enable and reinforce this type of behavior. It is their own fear of rejection, *their need* to be loved that fuels the inability to say no or to discipline a child.

This impulsivity can have some major consequences. If they drive too fast, drink, gamble, shop, etc., they will hurt themselves and the people that love them. It is not that they are just adrenaline junkies or have ADHD. The problem is that they don't have governors on their behavior. It seems that the part of the brain that says "don't go there; something might happen" just doesn't work or isn't fully developed. One study seems to suggest that the more a person uses drugs the more he or she damages the frontal lobe of the brain, the part of the brain that governs and moderates behavior. In fact, drug users operate more from the midbrain, an area that is more primitive and reactionary. If you're naturally impulsive and use drugs, you could be setting yourself up for a world of hurt. In some ways, impulsive types are perpetual adolescents. They might be fifty, but they have never grown up or learned to take on responsibility. If they have a criminal bent, they will find themselves in and out of the legal system throughout their lives.

These are just some of the negative styles or patterns of behavior we learn or adopt growing up. Sadly, there are many who are caught up in systems of thought that destroy families and relationships.

These patterns have led to a number of harmful ways that a person uses to cope with life. I am not trying to pass judgment on other people's lifestyles, but I do want to ask you if your lifestyle or view of life is working; if it is making you happy, and if you are getting what you want out of life.

The question is: Where do you go and what do you do when life isn't working? You might be a CEO, a leader in your church, or a leader in your community. Where can you go to admit your mistakes and look for help? Many of us have grave misconceptions about life.

You have to come to the point of asking yourself: Is what I am doing working? Is what I am doing making me happy? Do I feel alone? Is this thing called *life* working? Start by asking yourself these questions or looking at the things you have lost because of your style of coping.

I can list so many things: relationships, jobs, money, time, freedom, respect, time, etc. My coping style caused me to make bad choices, get into poor relationships, and, basically, shipwreck my life.

Proverbs 16:25 states: *"There is a way that seems right to a man but in the end it leads to death."*

This all relates to the questions that I asked earlier: What do you expect out of life? Do you expect to be hurt and ripped off? Do you trust no one? Do you expect to get your way every time you ask? What do you expect from reading this book? Will it just be another book on the shelf, or will it make a difference in your life? The point is that it is up to you—how you live out your expectations of yourself and others.

Second Corinthians 10:5 states: "We demolish argument and every pretension that sets itself up against the knowledge of God, and we take captive every thought to make it obedient to Christ."

Do you know what you really believe? Do you really know the truth about God?
Do you know that His power is real? Have you felt His presence in your life?

God is real, and His power is real. Jesus Christ is the same yesterday, today, and forever. He gives us power in His presence through His Holy Spirit. He works things together for good for those who love Him and are called to His purpose. He will never leave you or forsake you. He sets you free from the loneliness that you have within yourself. He lets you know that there is hope for the future. With God, there is always a future. The enemy wants to keep you isolated and stuck. He is the author of confusion. He wants to rob you of your faith and hope for tomorrow. He is a lair. But God has an answer. Greater is He that is in you than he that is in the world. He gives you the victory, which is your faith. His word. His presence sets you free.

Even if God closes doors in your life or if situations don't go as you expect, He can and will use even your mistakes for His purpose and glory. He will remind you that you are never alone. As Jesus said, "I am with you always, even unto the end of the age."

David said in Psalm120: "I cried to the Lord, and He heard me."

Jonah said, "I cried to the Lord and He heard me out of the belly of hell, and you heard my voice."

I have been to hell, so to speak, and God heard me, He was with me, and He used it for His glory.

In the span of one year, both of my parents died at a young age. In fact, my mother spent over nine months in and out of intensive care. She could only blink and nod her head. At the same time, I lost my career, my houses, and my family. More than that, I lost my hope and dreams for my family. I was even falsely accused of things I never did. My faith was tested. Have you ever been there?

But I can say like Job, "I know my redeemer lives." The Lord heard my cry; He put my feet upon the rock; He put a new song in my heart. He took all the hurt and pain in my life and turned it into my greatest blessing. What I thought was a curse became one of my greatest blessings. Through my trials, I was led to work with the young people that I have counseled for the last twenty-five years. What I thought ruined my life made me better and more effective. I learned real compassion. I have learned to trust Him more.

Psalm 37: "Trust in the Lord...Delight yourself in the Lord and He will give you the desires of your heart...The steps of a good man are ordered by the Lord... Though he fall, he shall not be utterly cast down for the Lord upholds him with His hand."

Psalm 27: "The Lord is my light and my salvation; whom shall I fear?"

Is your life changing around you? Do you feel that no one can hear your struggles? God hears what you can't say or what you don't know how to say.

Psalm 56 says, "He keeps my tears in his bottle; He writes them down in His book."

Are you stuck in the way that you deal with life and with issues? Do you feel trapped?

God hears; God knows; God wants to give you a fresh and new perspective—a new way of dealing with life. God wants to set you free from childish misconceptions and free you from the grip of the world's confusion.

Jesus said in John 16:33: *"I have told you these things, that you may have peace. In this world you will have trouble. But take heart, I have overcome the world."*

Chapter 2   Self Questions

1. How do you react to tough situations—for example: you just heard that your mother or someone you loved passed away? Would you self-medicate (get high), run away, get angry, etc.?

2. Are you stuck in the way you deal with issues? Is there a pattern? What have you done to cope in a way that others might say was crazy?

3. Is the way you cope or deal with life's problems working?

4. Do you keep getting hurt? If so, how?

5. Is the way you find happiness or get your needs met hurting you or other people?

6. What will it take to make you happy? Is it realistic?

7. What do you expect from other people? Is it being hurt, being lied to, or being used? Do you expect to be treated fairly? Is your motto in life: "Trust no man"? Why?

8. Do your expectations relate to your past history? Do your feelings today reflect your past?

9. Do you cause some of the drama yourself?

10. Look at yourself through the eyes of someone who loves you. What would they say to you? Or picture yourself sitting next to the child that was you— say, when you were five or six years old. What would you tell that child about his or her life and what he or she needs to know or how you feel about him or her?

Chapter 2   Homework

<u>Option 1</u>

I like to do an exercise in jogging your memory. Write on a piece of paper your first five or six memories of your life. I find that sometimes we can see the pattern of who we are by what we remember. Another way to do this is to write a short history of your life and the feelings that you had growing up. If you do this, the questions become: Are your memories correct, and how do these feeling and memories affect the way that you deal with things today? Could your memories be lying to you? If these memories are unpleasant, can you forgive yourself and others today? Do your memories give you unreal expectations of yourself and others?

Until we deal with these things, it is hard to get unstuck in our lives. It takes courage to look at our lives and see the truth of who we are and what we have become. It's like stepping on the scale in the doctor's office: many people just don't want to know. In fact, many people say things like: "I didn't have any problems until I went to the doctor or until I got into treatment."

<u>Option 2</u>

List the losses in your life. As you look at the list, what are your thoughts and feelings about those events? Do those losses affect the way you look at life today? Is your understanding of the past based in logic or on emotion?

Chapter 3

DEALING WITH DESTRUCTIVE DESIRES (ADDICTIONS)

Who or what is in control of your life? Is it your will? Is it God's will? Or do life's circumstances cause you to react the way you do? Do your needs and desires run your life? Are you being manipulated by the world that you live in? Or is what you are doing controlled by the will of God?

The apostle Paul tells us: *"I do not understand what I do. For what I want to do I do not do, but what I hate I do.... What a wretched man I am! Thanks be to God, who delivers me through Jesus Christ our Lord" (Romans 7:15ff).*

How many of us do or think things that we don't want to? How many of us are controlled by our emotions, our needs, our urges, or our destructive desires? How many of us overeat when we are not hungry or let our tempers or depression get the best of us? Maybe you drink too much or spend too much time controlled by the TV or the Internet. Some might call these our addictions, or "escapes."

> *The mind set on the flesh is death, but the mind set on the Spirit is life and peace, because the mind set on the flesh is hostile toward God, for it does not subject [take direction] to the law of God, for it is not even able to do so; and those who are in the flesh cannot please God.*
> —*Romans 8:6*

Paul here is sharing the heart of the Bible and its teaching. Many theologians would say that Romans 6, 7, and 8 are the pinnacle of biblical theology. Paul is talking here about his own inability to do the right thing when tempted by the power of sin and his flawed human nature. He is talking about what controls our lives. He complains that sometimes he does the very thing that he hates. (Don't we all sometimes?) In all of this, he comes to the understanding that in the forgiveness of Christ—in the power of the cross—we have true freedom from condemnation and judgment. By God's mercy and grace, through the indwelling of the Holy Spirit, we have the ability to overcome and be victorious in life.

Dear friend, Paul is saying that our problem isn't in our addictions or our destructive desires or urges. It is in how we think and react to things. It is not what is on the outside that controls us, but it is what is going on in the inside. The question is: Do we really know God and His power within us to overcome the situations in life? Do we really know the depth of His forgiveness and how it reaches into every corner of our lives? Do we know that He will make a way in all the struggles that we face? When you know God's purpose for your life and what He has freely given you through His presence and His Spirit, you can have joy and peace in any situation. He concludes chapter 8 with his stirring words of hope about God's love within our hearts:

> *For I am convinced that neither death nor life, nor angels, nor principalities, nor things present, nor things to come, nor powers, nor height, nor depth, any created thing, shall be able to separate us from the love of God in Christ Jesus our Lord.*

Paul speaks about God from what he knows and from what he has seen in his life. Can you? Can you see how God has brought you to the point of where you are in your life today? Maybe He is speaking to you today?

Within this chapter, Paul asks: What controls you? Are you controlled by your destructive desires and urges like hatred, sexual immorality, greed, etc., or are you led by the Spirit of God and love? It is the idea of contrasts:

- Self worship (idolatry) vs. God worship
- Lies vs. truth
- Hatred and anger vs. peace
- Sexual immorality vs. sexual purity
- The flesh vs. the Spirit
- A mind controlled by drugs (*sorcery* in the original Greek) vs. a mind submitted to God
- Fear vs. faith

The question becomes: What controls you? Is it your addictions, your vices, or your fears?

Paul says it is either the mind set on the flesh (animalistic human nature) or the mind submitted to the Holy Spirit, love, and peace.

Addictions

Before we go on, we need to ask the question: What is the "mind set on the flesh"? Some might say that it is a disease or a psychological problem or an addiction. Others say that it is just sin or the devil. Is it a symptom of another underlying issue? Is it an emotional, moral, or spiritual failing? Is it genetic or our flawed human nature? Or could it just be a failed coping skill we learned from how we were raised? Did I learn to be controlled by my anger by how I was raised—by what I saw or experienced growing up? I am tempted to say that it is all of the above.

I wish I knew an easy answer. One thing I know is that most people I have spoken with who are controlled by destructive desires or patterns in their lives all have *issues of guilt from their past* that have helped them to depend on a drug or an addiction in one form or another.

That is why I like what Paul says in Romans 8:1: *"Therefore, there is no condemnation for those in Christ Jesus...."*

In many ways, guilt and frustration lead a person to emotionally *withdraw* from society—to live in his or her own little world. I believe that the primary behavior of those controlled by impulsive destructive desires (addictions) is withdrawal or escape. In a sense, it is idolatry or self-worship. They would rather live in a fantasy world they create rather than the world God created. My question to you is: If you are controlled by selfish, destructive behavior, by anger, or by greed, what is it or who is it that you are escaping or running from? What hurts? What is it that you are afraid to face? Is it really God that you are running from? Think of it like this: Did the prodigal son disrespectfully take his inheritance and leave because he was angry with the father?

When did you give up hope in your life? Let's face it, most of us don't want to face our own struggles if we don't have to. That's where denial comes in. When we are controlled by our selfish desires, we are acting like children. Why do I say this? Because the way most people overcome addictions or these types of behaviors is by growing up. The majority of people who stop smoking do it on their own; the same is true about drug use or alcohol abuse. The point is that they grow up; they look at how their lives are going and finally choose to stop on their own. It is not the case for everyone, but it is true for the majority.

The sad thing I see is that some people get stuck in the stage of life that they were in when they started to run or escape. I have seen grown men in their fifties still acting like teenagers because they haven't dealt with their lives since their teens, or they haven't learned to cope with life. These people live in denial and passivity, stuck in seeing themselves as victims of society. They run from God. The problem is that they just don't see it. They might think that they are having fun—and they are for the moment—but reality always returns with feelings of rejection and loneliness. They can end up making promises they don't keep and failing in commitments. There is an old joke that asks, "How can you tell when a drug addict is lying?" The answer is, "When the addict moves his or her lips."

Romans 8:5 tells us that the mind controlled by the flesh—our sin nature, our destructive desires, and our impulses—is death. You might be able to live that way for a while, but life has a way of hitting you in the face. God has a way of getting your attention. Maybe it is when you lose your job or hurt because of a relationship with someone you love, or your health takes a turn for the worse because of all the things that you put your body through. Maybe it is when you have to face death. What are you going to do when you have to face reality or, in a sense, grow up? Sadly, some people never get the chance to truly live. I remember that it wasn't until my own father had to be confronted with death that he faced his own life and took responsibility for his actions and for his relationship with God. Only then did he find peace.

Are you struggling to deal with life? Do you seek ways to escape from reality or responsibility? Do people see you with a smile on your face, but inside you feel alone and detached, and no one knows the real you? All they see is what is on the outside, but inside, you hurt and can't admit your weakness. Do you hide yourself in work or distractions, spending hours on the Internet, or are you controlled by your anger or drinking or even porn? Is your life or your family falling apart? You might be a leader in your church or a boss on the job, but you are struggling on the inside? Have you believed the lies the world told you about happiness being fulfilled with self? Is your life sometimes a living hell? Are you really running from God? It wasn't until the prodigal son came to his senses—he changed the way he thought about his life, his father, and God—and then his life began to change. What will it take to hear that still small voice in your heart and to realize that you need to make a change? Only Jesus can calm the storm of your life. God has a way of stopping the drama in your life.

There are patterns in life that lead to death—death of self and death of relationships—but God wants to bless you. God created this world for our enjoyment. Too many people are stuck in a world of their own image and creation. That really is idolatry. They remind me of the dog that is stuck chasing his own tail or obsessing over a shadow or a ball. Only one thing, one obsession, or one desire seems to make them happy.

What is it that you truly care about? What do you spend your money on, or with what or whom do you spend your time? Look in your wallet; look at your monthly credit card statement, and that will tell you what is really important to you and what is running your life. The real question is: Why does the only thing that makes some people happy involve giving themselves brain damage (with drugs or drinking) or involve inflicting pain or hurting others?

Speaking from experience, I remember my parents fighting for years. First, I would go to my room and try to stay out of it. Over time I began using drugs to get away and to have some fun. And it was fun, but things never got better. I was still running until the point that I finally ran out the door, never to return to the family; and with that, the family dissolved. Again, as I stated earlier, this was my pattern: to withdraw. I would guess that the real underlying issue was depression or feelings of abandonment, fear, and loneliness. To this day, I find life at times to be a struggle, whether it means struggling to maintain a certain weight or to not be tempted with lust or greed or pride. We all get stupid, negative thoughts, but we don't have to follow them or give in to them. This all seems to be the human condition. Life is a struggle! But it doesn't have to overwhelm you.

Romans 8:16–18 tells us that God has given us His Spirit, to the point that we know in our hearts that we are His children, and we can call Him "Abba" (Daddy). He also promises us glory. We are going to see and be a part of His glory. How should that make us feel? From that truth, we know in our hearts that we don't have to be afraid of anything. Even as verse 36 of Romans 8 says, "We were as sheep to be slaughtered." He is saying that even in death, we win. Do you know that? Do you really know Him?

God and His Word and His presence can set you free from whatever controls you. He gives hope, and He gives direction. He lets you know that you are not alone, and that you are loved. He will never leave you or forsake you. He gives purpose for your life; in fact, He made you for a greater purpose. He will show up in the midst of your life, if you let Him. He gives you the victory, which is your faith, because greater is He that is in you than he that is in the world. You might be having struggles in life, but the Lord has a word for you:

you are not alone. So don't give up. David said, "I cried to the Lord and He heard my cry." In the midst of all the struggles in my life—from living on the streets and eating out of trash cans—God heard my cry. I cried to the Lord, and He put my feet on the rock. He put a new song in my heart. He changed my life; He will change yours.

The Bible teaches:

Psalm 27:1:

> "The Lord is my light and salvation: whom shall I fear? The Lord is the strength of my life of whom shall I be afraid?"

Psalm 46:1

> "God is our refuge and strength, a very present help in times of trouble."

Paul again tells us in Romans 8:26ff:

> "And in the same way the Spirit helps us in our weaknesses. For we do not know what we should pray...but the spirit intercedes according to the will of God...And we know that God causes all things to work together for the good to those who love God, to those who are called according to His purpose."

Ultimately, when we give in to the flesh, our sin nature, and our destructive desires, we lose our relationships—with God and with other people. Doubt, fear, and bitterness begin to run our lives, and we cut off God and the people we love. God gives us a free will to make choices in our lives. God respects your right to choose. But there is a way that seems right to a person, and that way leads to death. When our desires, selfish wants, needs, or fears take control of our lives, we miss out on God's blessings. Have you ever missed out on God's blessing by doing things your way?

The question really is: How do you deal with life? Do you self-medicate? Do you run away from problems? Are you overly controlling in life or in relationships? Are you run by your fears? Do your feelings control you? Do you continually do things that hurt yourself or others? Do you have to get the last word in an argument? Has your temper cost you your job, your friendships, or your marriage? Do you run up bills that you can't pay?

I am talking about using "things" that help you cope and take over your life that cause you harm in the long run. These can even be good things, like: work or religion or reading. But if they become an all-consuming escape or an excuse, then I would say that you have a problem. There is nothing wrong with working hard; in fact, it is a virtue. But if this virtue is the way you escape responsibilities or relationships with those you say you love, then I would say that it has become an addiction. It has become a destructive desire.

One psychiatrist friend shared with me the term "mastery." He said that we try to master the things that happened to us as children. For example, he said that if you were beaten as a child, at the time you were hit, in your mind you were saying to yourself: "Someday I'll do the beating; someday I'll be in control." Over the years, I have seen this play out in scary ways. I remember that in one group, a young man shared how his older female cousin raped him at the age of six. He shared how, within weeks of the incident, he raped his own sister. By the age of nine, he was stalking and raping other children. Not to justify his behavior, but was he in his own way subconsciously trying to get mastery of what had happened to him? I remember when I met a pretty, young nurse years ago. She told me that at the age of twenty-seven, she had already been married five times—each time to an alcoholic. Guess who the first alcoholic in her life was—her father. Who was she trying to control? Who was she really trying to master—her dad? The ironic thing was that we were working at a drug and alcohol treatment hospital when we met.

But the real question is: Are our strategies of getting control working? What will it cost us if we continue down that road? The problem is that we don't want to face how large the problem has become. It hurts too much to deal with our secret truths and to admit our mistakes or failures. I would guess that many of us don't know any other ways to cope. We might think that we don't have the ability to change things, but with the help of the Lord, we do!

The good news in all this is that God works all things for the good for those who love Him. He can and will use your mistakes for His glory. He will make your life a testimony of His love. You have a choice to let your past, your hurts, and your mistakes control your life, or you can use them to glorify God and help others. The truth is that God can and will get you out of any mess that you have gotten yourself into if you put your faith and trust in Him. In fact, He took mankind's greatest mistake, "the cross," and used it for His glory and our blessing. For that alone He deserves the praise.

The point is that your future is up to you. It is your choice and your decision. You might think that the future is all up to fate or even up to the Lord. But the Lord is waiting on you to make a choice to change—to trust in Him. If you do what you have always done, you will be where you have always been.

As Psalm 118 states:

1. *Oh give thanks to the Lord, for He is good! For His mercy endures forever...His mercy endures forever.*

5. *I called upon the Lord in my distress; and He answered me....*

7. *The Lord is for me; I will not fear; what can man do to me?*

8. It is better to take refuge in the Lord than, to trust in man.

9. It is better to take refuge in the Lord than to trust in princes [government].

13. I was falling, but the Lord helped me....

14. The Lord is my strength and my song and He has become my salvation....

22. The stone which the builders rejected has become the chief cornerstone....

24. This is the day that the Lord has made; let us rejoice and be glad in it.

29. Oh give thanks to the Lord! For His mercy endures forever.

The Self-Lies of the Carnal Mind

Many people with destructive desires or addictions can find all sorts of reasons and justifications to continue in their crazy behavior. It doesn't take much. They might be having a bad day, feeling stressed, or dealing with some sort of loss. On the other hand, it might be a great day, and things are going well, so there is a reason to celebrate. Either way, something within their thinking triggers their reactions.

Proverbs 23:7: *"As a man thinks so he is."*

What are the thoughts or lies that we tell ourselves that fuel dangerous desires (addictions) that rob our faith?

1. Everything-or-Nothing Thinking

These are times when we give 110 percent, but if something goes wrong or if we hear the word *no* or things don't go according to plan, we quit. How we react to the word *no* is an indicator of how well we handle life.

Over the years, if there is anything that stops a person from succeeding, it is this type of everything-or-nothing thinking. I am reminded of my son. When he was young, on Monday's I would cook pasta with a red sauce. My son decided that he didn't like the sauce, so I would suggest putting butter on the pasta. He said that if he couldn't have something different, he wasn't eating. I would say, "Fine, don't eat." Now that might be understandable for an immature kid who needs to grow up, but too many adults react the same way when life says no.

Let me relate this to a diet. Unless healthy eating becomes a lifestyle, we tend to binge and diet. It is feast or famine—everything or nothing. How many times do people go on a diet, lose the weight, and then gain the weight right back—and more? Or what about the addict who stops using drugs, but something goes wrong and that person quits his or her abstinence and falls right back to where he or she left off in his or her drug use. I have even seen the same behavior in church people. Something goes wrong, or their faith is tested, and they are out of the church; or worse: they turn their back on God forever. But this type of thinking is just self-pride—the kind of pride that comes before a fall. "It's my way or the highway." Again, this is idolatry. You set yourself up as God. You really don't want to listen to what God or anyone has to say about something. You are going to do things your way.

Life is not black and white; there is a lot of gray. Many of us have a hard time dealing with the ups and downs of life—the times we have to deal with the word *no*. But if we quit, if we take on the "I don't give a _____ attitude," we set ourselves up for failure. If we think, when overgeneralizing, that everything is bad or that nothing is good, then we can begin to feel sorry for ourselves. We can start to blame everyone and everything around us. We become the classic victim, seeing ourselves as having no control over our own lives. This can lead to frustration, and frustration leads to anger, and anger can lead to abuse of ourselves and others. Is that what happened in the case of Cain and Abel? Cain gave his offering—his "everything"—but it was not what God wanted. God said no to Cain, so Cain turned his back on God and adopted the "I don't give a rip, poor me" attitude and took his frustration out on his brother.

The real question is this: Where is the source of your strength? Is it in your faith in God—in your "love" for Him and others? Do you still have faith and hope when all hell breaks loose in your life and when life says no? God's love never fails. Do you know His love?

In Luke 18, Jesus tells of the widow who would not give up seeking the judge for help. He tells us to ask, to seek, to knock, and we will find. The idea is not to give up! Keep looking to God for the answer with relationships and situations. He will give the help.

"But you be strong and do not give up, for your work will be rewarded." —2 Chronicles 15:7

So what is the answer? It is realizing that not all of our thoughts are true. At times, we think all sorts of unreal emotional thoughts. *Emotions aren't always logical.* When we begin to feel sorry for ourselves or feel that we are the victims or that life is unfair to us, we set ourselves up for failure. But whoever said that life was fair, or that things should be easy? Most people who accomplish great things have had to overcome hard situations. That's really what makes their accomplishments so great. It is really all about control. If I quit, at least I am in control; I made the choice to stop trying. For some people it feels better to quit than to try and to fail. All of us have failures in life; all of us have to deal with things that are hard or unpleasant;

all of us hear the word *no*. Paul said, *"But one thing I do...I press on toward the goal...."* My point is this: we have a choice whether to quit or not. We can change our thinking and, therefore, our futures. Life is not so black and white or everything or nothing. In fact, "everything or nothing" is just a childish type of thinking.

2. Always-and-Never Thinking

There is another type of negative thought that can control your emotions. It is saying things to yourself like "I will *never* do better in life." "The boss is *always* out to get me." It is saying to yourself things like: "I *always* do poorly on tests, *always* fail, *always* get the shaft, *always* get lied to or cheated on," etc. Or it can sound like: "I can *never* get a break"; "I will *never* trust men/women because they always lie"; "I will *never* reach my dreams, *never* find someone to love me," etc.

Sometimes we believe the lies that we were told growing up, like: "You will always be a screw-up"; "you are just like your father; you will *never* be successful." These thoughts can affect your whole life. These are lies that we tell ourselves so that we don't have to take responsibility for our mistakes or our choices. These lies that we believe about ourselves and others stop us from living up to our full potential and choke God's blessings and peace from our lives. This causes us to limit God and His blessings.

Remember, *it is easier to believe a lie than to deal with the truth*. Always-and-never thinking is a way to blame the world and others *for our choices*. It is a false view of reality, and it can trigger anger and depression.

Sometimes we pray that people and situations would change but we really believe and act as if things won't change, *so they don't*. In this we ask ourselves: Where was God? But He was right there, waiting for us to step out in faith. We pray for circumstances and keep on believing: "I will never get a break"; "people will *always* treat me wrong." We feel that we have no options, no hope for the future. We feel stuck. We feel like quitting. We feel robbed or that life is unfair or that God is unfair or not hearing us. Believing things like *always* and *never* limits our potential blessings and faith.

But *"faith is the confidence in things hoped for...."* It is a confidence and trust in God. What are you hoping for? Where is your faith when it seems that God says no, and people hurt you? Are you struggling on the inside? Do you blame God or other people?

We can't control or change others, but we can get out of their way. We can think and react differently. We can change our situations and our feelings by changing our perspective. God is the master of change. There are new understandings and choices that we can make. Paul the apostle, in the midst of his greatest frustration, told us that when his prayers seemed unanswered, he could still say, *"My strength was perfected in weakness...that God's power may rest upon me" (1 Corinthians 12:5)*. He tells us that God's grace is enough. God gives enough grace for each day. He tells us to walk and live by faith and not by sight. Life has a way of humbling us, but by faith and God's presence in our lives, we have the ability to soar above life's circumstances or the lies that we were told or that we tell ourselves.

Until we let go of some of false expectations that we put upon God and others, we will not find peace. When we think in terms of "always" and "never" we forget God's grace and power. Remember, God was the one who used a few fish and loaves to feed thousands or a stone to bring down a giant. He still brings down giants today. He will give you what you need for your life. What you need to do is pray for the situation and beware of making sweeping generalizations about people and situations. It is the old saying, "Do your best and commit the rest." Too often we sit and wait for God, when God is waiting on us. We choose to trust Him and His authority; we choose to rejoice in Him and trust Him in spite of circumstances. Remember, it is the mind set on the Spirit that has life and peace. We need to check ourselves and our thinking and tell ourselves that something isn't *always* true or that it will *never* work.

How often do you use the words always *or* never? *Catch yourself next time! Try to take these words out of your vocabulary.*

Believing these lies is just another way to blame, justify, and make excuses. Blaming others is a sure way to set yourself up for failure. It makes an addict go back to his or her addiction. It causes a strong person to quit because he or she feels that he or she has no other choice. That individual believes that he or she can never win, or the he or she will always fail. Blaming gives you an excuse to not try. It gives control to the circumstances you face. In the long run, it can make you bitter about life and the world you live in. Worst of all, it will block your blessings and God's presence from your life. Of all the negative thought patterns, blaming is the most destructive. Jesus warns us about being critical and blaming:

Matthew 7:3: "Why do you look at the speck that is in your brother's eye, but do not notice the log that is in your eye? You hypocrite, first take the log out of your own eye and then you will see clearly…."

In contrast in the same sermon, Jesus said, *"Blessed are the pure in heart."* God is really concerned about the attitude of your heart. The truth is that only God can change your heart and your attitude. Only God can fill your needs and give real hope. He is the one who gives you power over circumstances of life. As Paul said, "When I am weak, He is strong" (1 Corinthians 12:9).

How often do you blame others, the past, or circumstances in which you feel you have no control for your life? Your past and your circumstances have made you who you are, and God will use it all for His glory if you let Him.

Blame can become what is called a *self-fulfilling prophecy*. Here is how it works.

If we think that no one in the world cares for us or that we will *always* be treated unfairly we will treat others in a negative way, and in return, they will treat us negatively, but we were the ones who set it up. We end up justifying our behavior to ourselves by blaming others.

Don't focus on all the *negatives*. Bring your situations to God. You need to trust God.

Paul tells us:

> *Yet in all these things [the trials of life] we are more than conquerors through Him who loved us. For I am persuaded that neither death nor life, nor angels nor principalities nor powers nor things present nor things to come. Nor height nor depth nor any created thing shall be able to separate us from the love of God which is in Christ Jesus our Lord."*
> *—Ro.8:37 ff*

He gives us enough grace for each day. Life might be beating you down, but trust God for what you know is true. You might be facing cancer or money problems, or your child or grandchild might be in trouble, but God doesn't give you more than He can handle. He will give you strength and wisdom. Of course, negative things happen; of course, everything in life is not always positive. But it seems that for many people, because of their past experiences, they tend to expect the negative and are continually disappointed. If we focus on the negative and if we focus on our mistakes, it will tend to rob us of our self-confidence.

The best example of this relates to playing the piano. Now I have played for more years than I want to count, but I have noticed that when you focus on the hard part of a piece of music, you can, as they say in sports, "choke" when you get to it. You are so busy focusing on how hard it is that the fear of hitting a wrong note causes you to freeze for a second. That hesitation causes you to make the mistake in musical time. The trick is to realize that it doesn't matter how hard it is, you have played hard pieces in the past, and so what if you make a mistake. In the long run, no one really cares; you have practiced, so play hard. In that, you gain momentum and confidence. It is better (at least in music) to play big and to play out large, and if you make a mistake, make it a big one. At least that is better than being afraid to play. It is the *fear* of failure and the fear of rejection that control us. In fact, I had a jazz instructor tell me once that if you make a mistake, do it again. They will think you planned it that way!

"Always-and-never" thinking is closely related to the *"everything-or-nothing"* way of thinking because it is a defense mechanism. It gives us an excuse to quit, to blame life, and to be controlled by fear. These overgeneralizations rob us of our faith and hope and deny God's power and grace.

In fact, always-and-never thinking is another way to take the blame off yourself and place responsibility for your life and how it turns out on outside forces. But others with worse circumstances have triumphed in life. This is only a way to justify yourself. Let's face it, it is hard to be real with yourself and others. This type of thinking basically gives you an excuse for your life and your behavior. It can give you the excuse to hurt others, steal from others, and do almost anything you want because it's someone else's fault.

3. If It Feels Good, Do It

Of all the destructive desires that can control your life, the desire to feel good—to only feel pleasure—can be the most destructive. Not that feeling good is wrong; it is just not the only reason to live. Only God can give real joy, purpose, and peace for your life. It is God who gives purpose and power to deal with circumstances in life. God created us that we might enjoy Him and the life He gave us. When we focus on what's above, we can deal with what's below. Other diversions are self-medication—or maybe I should say self-idolatry. For many years of my life, I would call myself a hedonist. I would seek pleasure and avoid pain, but in the end, all I felt was hurt and the feeling of being alone.

I think it has been since the '60s that the saying *"If it feels good, do it"* has captured generations. But it really doesn't work. Feelings are not always true, or at least they are not always logical. In fact, thinking with our feelings is not safe. Using drugs is an effective way to feel good for a moment, but in the long run, they could destroy your life. Whenever you have a strong feeling about something good or bad, you need to stop and think it through; you need to ask questions and get more of the facts. Battles are won and lost by not knowing or denying the truth. Being controlled by our destructive desires will lead us away from God and the people we love.

The Bible tells us to not be ignorant. Ignorance is not bliss; it is dangerous. If we listen to the musings of the world around us, we can be carried away by our own selfish desires and, like Adam and Eve, lose paradise. Remember, the Bible says that God tempts no person; we are drawn into sin by our own flesh and human weakness. If we listen to some college professors who are more interested in hearing their own hedonistic ideologies and feeling important, we will fall for whatever they sell us. If we listen to the media and its advertising, we will be made to feel "less than" others, and our insecurity, greed, and imposed need will take over. In the end, we lose fellowship with God and our loved ones. Ignorance is no excuse.

In fact, sometimes doing the thing that doesn't feel good for the moment is better for you. Exercise and diet are examples of that. I can think of disciplining my children. It doesn't feel good to tell them no and see them get upset but I have to. Our culture tells us these days that feelings are everything; to feel good is the goal of life. That is a lie too; often because one partner doesn't "feel in love" for the moment, a family gets destroyed. The mind set on the flesh (the carnal) is death. Instead of seeking the pleasures of the world, we really need to seek God, but that doesn't seem logical.

> *The person without the Spirit does not accept the things that come from the Spirit of God but considers them foolishness, and cannot understand them because they are discerned only through the Spirit.* —1 Corinthians 2:14

Let's face it: spiritual things don't make sense to the natural mind. The natural mind worries about what others might think, what others have, feeling good, and keeping up with the Joneses. The spiritual mind worries about what God thinks. When you only have two days off a week, going to church doesn't make sense. Giving your hard-earned money to a ministry and trusting God makes no more sense to the natural mind than walking on water. Paul said that the cross (our faith) is foolishness to those who are perishing. It takes the Spirit of God to change a heart and a mind. *"Has not God made foolish the wisdom of the world?" (1 Corinthians1:20b).*

A good general knows that diversion is important in winning a battle. Realize this: the enemy will get you so busy running after the things of the world and being accepted by those in the world so that he can attack you in the areas that are most important: your faith and your relationships with those you love. He will get you so busy looking at what you don't have that you forget what you do have. Romans 8 says that we are God's children and His heirs. Jesus said that he came that we might have life and have that life more abundantly. The Bible tells us that He calls us—that we were handpicked by God. It tells us that the future is in His hands. Our future will be better than our past. The point is that with God, we don't need anyone else's approval. The point is that God loves us and wants to bless us. He has blessed us; He has set us free from sin and death, and nothing will separate us from His love.

Solomon was a man who had everything the world had to offer. For years he led by feelings of hedonistic pleasure. In the end, he found no real satisfaction in anything other than God. He tells us these thoughts:

I said to myself, "Come now, I will *test you with pleasure. So enjoy yourself.*" And behold, *it too was futility.* I said of laughter, "It is madness," and of pleasure, "What does it accomplish?" I explored with my mind how to *stimulate my body with wine* while my mind was guiding me wisely, and how to take hold of folly, until I could see what good there is for the sons of men to do under heaven the few years of their lives. I enlarged my works: I built *houses* for myself, I *planted vineyards* for myself; I *made gardens and parks* for myself and I planted in them all kinds of fruit trees; I made *ponds* of water for myself from which to irrigate a forest of growing trees. I bought male and female slaves and I had home born slaves. Also I possessed *flocks* and herds larger than all who preceded me in Jerusalem. Also, I collected for myself *silver and gold* and the treasure of kings and provinces. I provided for myself male and female *singers* and the pleasures of men—*many concubines.* Then *I became great* and increased more than all who preceded me in Jerusalem. My *wisdom* also stood by me.

All that my eyes desired I did not refuse them. I *did not withhold my heart from any pleasure,* for my heart was pleased because of all my labor and this was my reward for all my labor. Thus I considered all my activities which my hands had done and the labor which I had exerted, and *behold all was vanity and striving after wind* and there was no profit under the sun. "Vanity of vanities," says the Preacher, "all is vanity!" In addition to being a wise man, the Preacher also taught the people knowledge; and he pondered, searched out and *arranged many proverbs.* The Preacher sought to find delightful words and to write *words of truth correctly.* The words of wise men are like goads, and masters of these collections are like well-driven nails; they are given by one Shepherd. But beyond this, my son, be warned: *the writing of many books is endless, and excessive devotion to books is wearying to the body.*

The *conclusion,* when all has been heard, is: *fear God and keep His commandments,* because this applies to every person.

—Ecclesiastes 2:1–11; 12:8–13, emphasis mine

In many ways, the enemy wants to steal your faith, your love, and your relationships with your family. He will get you striving after feeling good and getting things—houses, cars, money, pleasure, and position—all the while attacking the real foundations of a happy life. Too often we forget all the things that we have been feely given through the Spirit in Christ. We get sidetracked by the world and its pleasures.

Feelings aren't always right or wrong; they are just feelings. Within life, we have to face all sorts of unpleasant feelings: whether it is the loss of a parent or job or health, etc. It seems that we live within a culture that wants to pretend that things will always be easy and good. Living happily ever after is a fairy tale. Life is filled with tears. It is the addict or the person run by desires who doesn't want to face it or who doesn't know how to face it. Each day I am astonished by the resilience of people who overcome tragedies. It is our choice. We need to learn to mourn and accept the losses and move on with life. Unfortunately, it is the addict, through his or her addiction, who cuts himself or herself off from family and communities that will help that person deal with the unpleasant feelings of life. The question is: Why do I feel this way, and what can I do about it? It's asking yourself: Is the way I am feeling logical?

4. The Lie of Taking Things Personally

Dear friend, it is important to guard your heart. If the enemy is to be successful, he will get you to stop loving and to stop trusting. He will get you to take other people's problems and issues personally. He will let you get your heart broken so that you lose your faith. If we lose love and faith, we lose the power in our lives. This is when we lose love in our marriages or in our relationships in our attempt to protect ourselves. We cut ourselves off others so that we don't get hurt, but we also cut off God. It is a sacrifice of faith to open ourselves up to God's love and the imperfect love of others.

Too often we get hurt over situations that have nothing to do with us. How many times have we gotten our feelings hurt by someone else who says something to us in a negative way? But that is who and what they are—negative and bitter people. That is not about you but more about them. The truth is that they just might be having a bad day. You might be the person who got in the way. One boss told me years ago at a board meeting when one person was being a bit surly, "I guess he just didn't get laid last night." Unfortunately, there is some truth to that thought.

It even gets worse when the person who treats you poorly is a family member. They are supposed to love you, but they just might not know how. That's not your fault. I have seen so many people get angry over the fact that a parent didn't love them. They take it out on everyone around them. Would you be upset or feel robbed if your parent was born blind? No! Then why do you get upset when a parent doesn't know how to love you or themselves? The truth is this: that parent just can't see it; he or she might not have ever dealt his or her own issues to be able to love. But you take it personally! The question is: Can we mourn or accept the loss and move on? Can you say to yourself that you might not have the love you needed from this person, but the love of God is enough? Is God's love enough? Can you realize that others can't give you what they don't have and realize that you didn't do anything wrong? Some of you have been through all sorts of hurt in your lives, through no fault of your own. You know that if it wasn't for the love of God, you wouldn't be here; you would have never made it. For that you praise can Him.

5. **The Lie of Conformity**

Romans 12:2 states:

> And do not be conformed to this world, but be transformed by the renewing of your mind, that you may prove what is that…perfect will of God.

Too often I hear people tell me that everyone is doing this or that. We justify speeding if we believe everyone does it and gets away with it. Advertising uses this type of thinking to get us to buy one thing or another. We live in a world where we are constantly comparing ourselves and conforming to the group.

People have been conforming to group ideologies from the beginning of time. We innately jockey for position within our societies and groups, and much of this involves conforming to group or societal norms. Is it because we all want to fit in and be loved? If we think that everyone has this or that, we are compelled to think that we need it as well. In fact, if we believe that everyone thinks this or that idea, we will, in general, conform our thinking to the group. In a sense, we begin to believe that something is wrong with us if we think differently. For something to be different. transformation needs to happen within our souls. It is in the realm of the spirit first that real change takes place. Will we listen to the voices around us, or will we trust God? Will we hear the Word of God? Will He touch our souls? Faith comes by hearing and hearing from the Word of God. It is your choice to hear.

Do we really believe that it is important to keep up with the Joneses? It takes a strong individual to stand up to a group or to disagree with the majority. But with you and God, it is a majority. Groupthink and pressure will cause an individual to do things that he or she wouldn't do alone. In my travels, I have spent time in Germany. Having a Jewish background, at first I really did not have comforting thoughts for the German people. The truth is that I found them to be warm and hospitable. So how could they commit such atrocities during the war? With Nazi control of the media and every aspect of life, it would have been hard to have stood up against the tide. It has been shown that of all the people that rescued the Jews, they all had one thing in common: they were nonconformists. Groups can cause us to do right and can cause us to do wrong.

One person by himself or herself might not get into trouble, but if that individual sees himself or herself within a group, he or she will tend to follow the group into whatever activity (good or bad) that they get involved with. Is that how mobs or rioters tend to follow without thinking? Generally, by themselves they would not do things that they would do within a group. For those in the addiction world, if they return to the old places and friends, they also fall into the old behavior. The truth is, you are who you hang with.

"Do not be deceived: Bad company corrupts good morals" (1 Corinthians 15:33).

The key is to develop new peer groups and associations that reinforce a healthy lifestyle. My point is for you to trust in the Lord. He is greater than any group or ideology. He controls the destiny of nations and of your life. As you follow Him, He will give you divine protection and help. He will deliver you from the empty promises of joy, power, or satisfaction that the world offers. *"Trust in the Lord with all your heart and lean not on your own understanding and He shall direct your paths" (Proverbs 3:5–6).*

6. The Problem of Conditioning

Most people have heard about Pavlov and his experiment with his dogs: how he would feed them each day and ring a bell. Then one day at dinnertime, he just rang the bell, and the dogs began to drool. The dogs associated the bell with food. I believe that it is much the same with drugs or other addictions. The addict associates them with pleasure. I have sat in a room and shown a video containing a certain drug. The response was that almost every user in the room had a big smile on his or her face. Just looking at the picture made him or her want to use. Can you remember your favorite food growing up? Once you began to smell it, you could taste it. I think it is the same with drugs: once you see or smell them, you can begin to feel them ever so slightly. This can put you into a craving state. Just the thought or memory of the feeling is enough to get you to act out compulsively. One study showed that when addicts were shown videos of people using, their brains (during an MRI scan) lit up or showed more activity than when shown pornographic material.

To put it simply I call this *"the smile of death."* Some years ago I saw a film called *24 Hours on Crack Street.* The reporter was interviewing a woman who seemed to be living on the street. She stated that she had abandoned her children and was just doing whatever she had to do to get by. She looked depressed, but suddenly her demeanor changed before taking a hit as she held up a crack pipe. Across her face beamed a wide smile. It was as if everything was going to be good, and she could not access the information of her own misfortune. Through the years I have seen this smile on many lost and hurting faces.

One other aspect of this that needs to be addressed is the fact that daily use of some drugs can damage the parts of the brain where the feelings of joy happen. Dopamine (the chemical in the brain that produces good feelings) is short-circuited to the point where it is hard for the brain to function properly or to experience happiness without the drug. In the long run, it takes more and more of the drug to, in a sense, rejuice the joy. As the brain is damaged in many areas through drug use, the ability to cope with day-to-day problems and life suffers as well. This inability to cope leads to more stress and the greater need to self-medicate, thus reinforcing the cycle of drug abuse. Drugs, it seems for some, become the only way that a person knows how to enjoy life.

Think of it like this: We know that strawberries taste sweet, but if you eat sugary candy before eating the strawberry, it seems as if the strawberry is tasteless. For many, after using drugs, the simple things of life that naturally bring joy just don't feel as satisfying. Life is no longer sweet without the drug. Studies seem to show that the brain has the ability to heal if a healthy lifestyle is implemented. This is not always the case: for some, the use of drugs brings on schizophrenia. I have seen friends who never came back. When stressed, they heard voices. I have seen those that have stopped using, but the voices continued. They ended up living on the streets.

The Spiritual Issue

People are spiritual creatures. We are made in the image of God, and God is a spirit. God is spiritual; God is creative. No matter what you believe, I would say that you are spiritual; you're creative, and you dream for things beyond yourself. Man has a soul that yearns for God. We yearn for something beyond ourselves to give us meaning and definition. There is this need within us. It is a part of who we are. Now you might say that you don't believe in God or even know if there is a God. Even this line of thinking takes faith. It takes faith to believe in nothing. It takes faith to believe that we evolved from nothing—as much as it takes faith to believe in a Creator. It takes faith to believe in the inherent good of mankind; it takes faith to trust in the state to care for our needs. It takes faith to believe in communism or socialism or whatever "ism" you hold to. Every religion and every belief system takes faith.

What does this have to do with addiction? It has to do with many of us because in our spiritual and fallen nature we seek something to believe in beyond ourselves. Is that why we attach ourselves to a sports team, group, or ideology? We seek another identity or reality to get us away from the struggles of life; we seek things beyond ourselves. Is this a part of our spiritual need? Whether it is in drug use or escapism by watching too much TV or gambling or whatever, we seek to fill the hole within our soul or the hurts in our lives with something else. Truth is, at least from my perspective, that hole can only be filled with God.

You might ask how that is different from an addiction. Carl Marx said, "Religion is the opiate of the masses." For some, religion or religiosity is an addiction and an escape from reality. Religious addictions—or maybe I should say "religious crazy"—can be one of the worst addictions. People murder their own children in the name of God. But a real relationship with God should cause us to look at ourselves and see where we are lacking and where we need to be more like Christ. Jesus said, "You will know them by their fruit," which means from their actions (from the Hebrew perspective). What do your actions say about your relationship to God? The Bible isn't an escape, but it is a mirror to hold your life up to. Understanding God's grace causes a true believer to want to improve his or her behavior, attitude, and relationship with others as well as God. If faith causes no real change of heart and action, I have to wonder if the so-called spiritual relationship is real.

As the Scripture says, the real relationship with God involves *"doing justice [right actions], loving mercy, and walking humbly with your God" (Micah 6:8).*

My Personal Example

I spent ten years using all types of drugs on a daily basis. I found that it didn't work, and I was still unhappy with myself. Even after becoming a Christian, for the first few months, I still used small amounts of marijuana. It didn't help my Bible study because I had to read things over and over again while I was stoned. I didn't see anywhere in the Bible that said, "Thou shall not smoke weed." I think many so-called "Christian" drug users justify their use this way.

It all came to a head one evening when I was at a friend's house. Everyone was getting high, and as was generally the case, my hand was slightly shaking. This was normal for me. There was a crowd there because the band that I was in was rehearsing. A friend was in the next room having sex with a woman. People were laughing and talking about the woman in a derogatory way. Suddenly, I realized that they were speaking about an old friend's wife and a mother of three. I had not seen her in at least five years. Then a thought came into my head: "This isn't of God." It might sound simplistic, but I thought that if it isn't of God, then it must be of the "other guy." Then a verse from the Bible came into my head, and I don't believe in coincidence. It was from the Book of Jude, where Michael the archangel was fighting for the body of Moses. Michael, knowing he was not strong enough, said to Satan, "The Lord rebuke you." So I said those words as I prayed silently, and suddenly my hand stopped shaking, and I never returned to drugs. That was 1977, and I have never relapsed.

I do believe that there is a spiritual realm that influences us. I am not saying that every person who does drugs is demon possessed. What I am saying is that there are spiritual realities that influence us. Let's face it. Everyone who does drugs or gets drunk is seeking another reality. That other reality is real, and I believe it has power. I call it the spiritual realm. It can influence people for the good or the bad. Have you heard those voices? Again, it is your choice to go there. I don't blame people who want to escape, but escape to where? The question is who or what controls or influences your mind? Is it God or the other guy? Is it fitting into the culture around you? Is it being a part of some group, or does the need to get high and escape sum up your life? I have seen parents abandon their children for drugs, or spend their food money to feed their addiction. I have seen young people rob their parents to get high. God wants to give you the power to beat any addiction. He alone can heal your soul. It is up to you. He can give you rest.

In spite of all your blessings in life, does life still make you crazy? Do you believe life will never get better? Do you want to quit? Do you feel like running away?

As I have said before, it is easier to believe a lie than to deal with the truth. You see, the problem really is in the way that we think about things. If you are struggling for joy in your life, then maybe it is time to change your mind about some things. Maybe the things you think that will make your life better or happy really don't. Maybe having more possessions or money or that new relationship or a new pill will not make things right. The emptiness always returns. In fact, maybe some of the things that you strive for are the very things that are robbing you of your peace.

The power is in the changed mind, the changed way of thinking. It is in the presence and the reality of God in your life that there is freedom and power. It means God helps us if we submit, to getting rid of that old way of thinking and dealing with things. It is letting go of old hates, jealousies, defenses and fears. It is the mind set on the flesh that traps us. Sometimes it is the things we think we "need" or desire that destroy us. Until our faith comes to the place of our hurts, fears, frustrations and failures we will waste years of our lives continually getting hurt or hurting others.

Friend, you were not created to be controlled by your destructive desires. There is greatness in you because you were made in God's image, flawed as you might be. You were called before the foundations of the world to be His child. Don't waste your life going in circles, stuck in ways that don't work. Don't believe the lies of the enemy that you can't change, that you can't grow, or that life cannot be better. With God, opportunity is ahead. Praise Him today for what *He will* do your life.

The point is that your future is up to you. It is your choice, your decision. You might think that the future is all up to fate or even chance. You might think the deck is stacked against you. But the Lord is waiting on you to make a choice to change and to trust in Him. If you do what you have always done, you will be where you have always been.

Chapter 3   Self Questions

1. What is addiction? How do you think or feel about using drugs? Are your thoughts automatic? Is it logical to think this way?

2. How might addiction be emotional withdrawal? If so, what are you running from? When did you lose hope in your life? What happened?

3. Could your addiction be a coping skill or a defense mechanism based in fear?

4. Are there issues behind addictions?

5. How do you deal with problems? Do you self-medicate?

6. What is the biggest problem you face? How do you deal with it?

7. Is there something that controls you—like your anger? What pushes your buttons or frustrates you the most in life?

8. Do you quit when things go wrong, or do you try harder? Do you think bad things will always happen? How does that make you feel? Explain.

9. Do you take things personally? If yes, what things? Is it logical? Does it work?

10. Do you go along to get along? Are you a follower? How do you choose who to follow? Why or why not? Give examples.

11. How has addiction worked in or influenced your life?

Chapter 3   Homework

1. Make a list of how many times you use the words *always* or *never* within one week.

2. Make a list of how often you blame others.

3. Write down the last time you took something personally. Write how it turned out.

4. Write down your feelings on growing up in your home and how they affect you today.

Option 2

List your negative thoughts for the week.

Next to each thought, write how it might it be a lie. Rewrite the thought in a positive way.

Examples: "I always get lied to" versus "I am a smart person; I know who has my back and who doesn't."

"I am stupid" versus "I make mistakes—everyone does—but I just work harder and make it right."

Keep a list of your positive thoughts and read them daily.

Chapter 4

TOUGH PEOPLE LAST; TOUGH TIMES DON'T

(Lead Us Not into Temptation)

I remember when I was young. I thought that I had all the answers. I thought that I knew more than my teachers, my parents, and the culture. Such were the '60s. Then life happened. I went through one crisis after another. I realized quickly that I wasn't as smart as I thought; in fact, I felt lost, alone, and confused. In fact, I was contemplating suicide. Have you ever been there?

What do you do when life hits you on the head, when you lose your job, or when the child that you prayed for and hoped for miscarries—when things don't go as you expect? Do you get depressed? Do you want to give up? Is that when you feel like praying? Maybe it is just one word: *help*. Jesus taught us to pray.

"Lead us not into temptation, but deliver us from evil for Thine is the kingdom and the power and the glory forever amen" (Mathew 6:13).

When things go wrong, can you trust in the Lord and trust in His power and glory? The truth is that some of the things in my life that I thought were a curse or a tragedy have become the greatest blessings in my life. Things really do work together for the good. Praise God.

Think about this for a minute: Jesus begins His ministry by going out to meet John the Baptist, where He is baptized, and coming out of the water there's a voice from heaven saying, "This is my beloved son in whom I am well pleased." Following that, the Spirit, the Holy Spirit of God, led Jesus out into the wilderness to be tempted. This is where Jesus faces the devil in all his power and trickery. After Jesus had a great start in his ministry, his life takes a sharp turn into the desert.

Are you in a desert in your life? Are you running on empty? Our text comes from the greatest sermon that was ever preached, "The Sermon on the Mount." In the middle of that sermon, we see Jesus teaching his famous prayer. He tells us to pray these enigmatic words, "Lead us not into temptation."

What does it mean to be tempted? And are we tempted by God? What is this thing called temptation? Does God want us to be tempted?

Let me say this: temptations can creep into your life secretly, when you are not looking. They can come in the midst of when things are going wrong. We can be tempted after things are going right or after a great victory of faith and blessing from God. Right after Jesus heard the words of His Father, "this is my beloved son," it was then that He was led into the wilderness to be tempted.

Temptation can be hidden behind the smile; it can hide behind wonderful clothes and an outward appearance. Temptation can be in the heart and in the greed of a rich man or in the envy of the poor man. It can ride to work with you, and if it doesn't come with you, it can catch a ride on the way home.

Temptations are really trials. We talk about trials and temptations, and in the original language the word *temptation* has the idea of a trial, a test, and in the sense that Jesus is saying, pray that the trials of life don't come upon you. Pray that your faith is not tested by the enemy like Job's was. This is probably how I might pray: "Lord, please don't give me more than I can handle." (It's the prayer of my heart that I would go before one of my children.) Haven't you prayed that? Yet, "all God's children got problems; we all have trials and temptations." I believe the greatest temptations or trials are on the inside: how I think about something. It starts within my fallen human nature to want things my way and not God's way.

Trials can come into a small one-bedroom apartment in the ghetto, where people are just struggling to get by to make ends meet. Trials can come in a middle-class home. Trials can show up in the form of depression at the morning breakfast table in between coffee and pancakes and grab you right there. They can come in the form of a phone call in the middle of the night or as a report from the doctor. They can come to the house of the affluent as you are sitting in your Jacuzzi or hot tub.

It can be *that little voice* in your head that tells you that "*life isn't worth living.*" It's that little voice that says, "There's no God," or "He doesn't love you." It's the whisper of discouragement that says, "Why do you keep on trying? You're just a loser!" It's the thought that says, "Life will never change; you will always be weak; you will always have things go against you. No one will ever love you; you'll never get ahead." It tells you, "You will never get out of what you have gotten yourself into." All of these are lies that we tell ourselves.

You see, *the greatest test or trial is on the inside. It is what happens between the ears. It is in the mind.* It isn't just what happens on the outside; it is what happens on the inside and the way you feel about it that determines success or failure. It is like those cartoons you saw when you were little: the person has a little devil on one shoulder and a little angel on the other. The question is which one will he or she listen to?

Depending on the circumstances around me some days, *people get the devil and not the angel.* Some days I can have a bad thought in my head, and it can color my day for hours, maybe even days. Some days the worst things come out of my mouth, or wrong thoughts still get in my head. You see that the real trial, the real temptation, is on the inside. It can cause you to make bad decisions that can affect your family and life forever. The way you deal with a trial can shape your life and the life of the generations that follow you.

A trial and temptation can be so powerful that it can fill you with envy and make life seem so bitter. The ancient Jews in the time of Christ spoke about an evil eye—a bad eye. This was a person filled with greed, pride, and jealousy. This individual's attitude colors everything he or she looks at. That is why Jesus tells you to tear out your eye if it causes you to stumble.

As a Christian, you can look at the world with a bitter evil eye as well. We see some people prosper in a way that seems like everything comes easily. *They don't try; they don't even honor God or pray.* In fact, it seems that they are against God, but they are blessed anyway, and it seems that they are given more. It is as if God has a bad sense of humor that they prosper in their evil right in your face. Their victories are in your face, and while you are going through some agony, their success is in your face to the point that you despair of life. This truth led David to say in Psalm 37: *"Fret not of evil doers who prosper along the way; they shall soon be cut off."*

David is saying that you should not just jump to conclusions or make an impulsive decision about life in the midst of a trial or in the midst of your frustration or temptation. His point is this: "don't look at the short run. Look at the long run. Look at things through the truth of the Lord. Look at the long-term consequences of behavior and decisions." In other words, "hang in there; you don't yet see the end of the situation." He is telling us to trust in the Lord. In the midst of the trial, trust in the Lord; trust Him when life seems unfair. He is telling you to continue to do the right thing. He is saying that what goes around comes around. God will not be mocked.

Jesus said, *"Lead us not into temptation."* Lead us not into the trial. In fact, I get frustrated at times when I read the words of James, who tell us to "count it all joy when you encounter various trials." Why would God allow us to encounter trials and temptations? I thought that He loved us. But James also tells us that, "God tempts no man," and that we are carried away by our own lusts, our own flawed human nature.

The truth is that yes, I am saved. My soul is with God; I am seated in the heavenly realm with Christ, but my mind is still being transformed daily into the mind of Christ. My mind is also influenced by the world, the culture, the family that I live in or that I was raised in, and, of course, by my fallen, human sin nature. That's right I am. I am a sinner—just ask my wife or, better still, my kids.

Why does God allow us to be tempted? Because it is in the midst of the trial that *great things happen.* It is in the midst of the trial that we are pushed to a higher level of faith. For some it was a trial that brought us to your knees to accept Jesus as our Lord and Savior. It was a trial that pushed us to a higher step of faith. It was only in the trial that *the prodigal son* saw how much he needed and loved his father. It is in the trial that God leads us, molds us, and changes us. That is why the church has always flourished in persecution. Dear friend, just because you got saved doesn't mean that God is done with you yet. Sometimes He has to push us and squeeze us like a tube of toothpaste to get us to change—to mold us into who we need to be.

In fact, the truth be told, every trial is an opportunity for growth and change. That's why Paul can say, *"It is not that I have reached it, but one thing I do; I press on to the goal, the prize, the upward call of God." I press on*, no matter what the world says. *I press on* no matter what society says. *I press on* no matter what my friends or family say. *I press on.* Keep pressing on toward your goal, your hope, your dream that God has put in your heart. Dear friend, *a trial or temptation is just a step along the way to where you are going,* to where God is leading you. Are you someone who is going through a trial—a struggle where God might be speaking to you?

Dear friend, *it is after the trial,* after we face the fears, after we learn to trust God no matter what—that's when the blessings come. It is after the pain that the baby is born. When the opposition comes, that's the time when you have to bear down; that is when you have to stand your ground. Don't worry about the opposition or what the world may say. Don't worry about being politically correct. Don't compromise your identity, your faith, and your uniqueness to fit into the world that you live in. Don't worry about what the crowd may say. *If God has promised* you something in His word—if God has said this is true, then it is. There is nothing that anyone can do to stop or take away from God's promise and God's truth.

That's when you need to take a stand for what you believe in. That is when you have to trust; that is when you have to believe. It is darkest before the dawn; it is pain before the birth. Pain is an indication the birth is getting close. Stay true, stay strong, and stay focused on God, and these things— your needs —will be added unto you.

You might be facing all sorts of trials—financial, physical, marital—but this is the time that you can't give up; you must stay strong. You have to believe that there is something within you worth fighting for. There is something within your soul, your faith, and your future that is worth fighting for. It is bigger than any of the problems of this life.

Are you about to open the door to something new and wonderful?

It was in the midst of a trial that a young boy confronted a giant and said, "Who is this uncircumcised Philistine to taunt...the living God?" And that boy became a king. It was in the midst of a trial, one of the darkest times in history, when one man said, "We shall defend our island whatever the cost maybe. We will fight them on the beaches; we shall fight them on the landing ground; we shall fight them in the streets; we will never surrender." And the truth is, "This was their finest hour." In another time of trial, another man said, "Ask not what your country can do for you but what you can do for your country." (That type of thinking has gone by the wayside today.) And another one said in the midst of a Cold War, "Mister Gorbachev, tear down this wall." And there was a birth of freedom heard around the world.

Dear friends, it is after the trial that you can look back and see where God has guided you, where God has directed you, and where He has been by your side. It was through the trial that God turned the cross into the crown, the agony into the ecstasy. You don't appreciate good health until you have experienced bad health. You don't appreciate what you have until it is gone. You don't thank God for the good until you have been through the bad. It is through the trial that you gain strength. It is through the trial that you truly learn to thank the Lord and rest in Him. It is through the trial that you learn perspective. It is in the midst of the trial that you truly learn how to pray and seek the Lord.

Sadly, for many of us, we call on the Lord when we are afraid and when we can see no other help. But we forget Him once life gets back to normal and when life gets back to the point that we think we can handle things on our own. In that, we set ourselves up to go through the trial again.

Jesus tells us to pray "lead us not." This implies that God is directing us throughout our lives. God is guiding us, moving us to fulfill His purpose. We are "in process"; we have not arrived at the promised land yet. This creates tension in our lives: we know what God has in store for us, and we know that He will bless us, and that in the future, we will be with Him forever, only to wake up to deal with the reality of the struggle of what is today.

This brings us to the next part of the text, where Jesus tells us to pray "deliver us from evil." We live in world where many don't believe that evil or a devil exist. In fact, it is logical to say this if you don't believe there is a God. Without God—let me say it again—*without God there is no evil.* Where there is no truth, there is no right or wrong. In the modern university education, there is no single belief system better than another (except if it is Christianity). Evil, the devil, and even God are a myth. Everything has no meaning—no importance. When you're dead, you're dead; that's it. But tell me this, how else other than "there is a devil, and there is evil" can you explain a child aborted every thirty seconds? Or seventy million killed in China? Or the fifty million within Stalinist Russia? Or the Holocaust? Or the genocide in Rwanda? Or the killing of Christians in the Sudan or within the Middle East today?

The question is to whom or what are you really committed?

If there is anything that the devil would like to steal from you, it is your faith and love for God and others. You can't live the victorious life *without love*; your life becomes a lot of noise when the desire of things and power rule your life. Like the seed that grows up among the thorns, it will choke you and rob you of every blessing. It will rob you of the joy and love that God has for you and the love that you have for others because selfishness becomes all consuming. There is never enough, and we always want more. We get so consumed in building our kingdoms in this world. Jesus instinctively must have known this because in His text He tells us that we can't love God and money. Dear friend, the greatest trials that you will face are greed and the love and want for self. I want things my way, and I want them now. You can never fill the hurts or the needs of your life without God. You see, the devil will get you looking at what you don't have, and it will rob you of being thankful for what you have.

How do you define yourself? Is it by the designer clothes you wear, the car you drive or the house you live in? Is it because you don't know who you really are and what you really believe that you attach yourself to things? Is it because you don't know who you are, and you don't know the God you serve? Jesus says that you are so much more than things. Styles change, and clothes wear out; your sports team will lose, but God's word, His truth, and His love are forever. When you know God, you don't have to seek approval in what you have or who you hang with. Joy comes from knowing Him and His love.

What is real holiness? Is it going to church seven days a week? Is it giving your money to God or fasting? No! It is being different on the inside. It is being different from the world and society and the way the world thinks about life. It is being separate for God—separate in how you react and how you think. No matter what the world says, you press on toward the goal, the prize, and the call. You don't worry about what they may say or what they may do. Do you know in your heart what God has promised you? It is being different on the inside. It is having love in your heart and not anger. It is having love in your heart rather than revenge. 1 John 4:7b says, *"Everyone who loves is born of God and knows God."* Again, it is about the attitude of the heart—the way you think on the inside. That's why Jesus, in the same sermon, talks so much about forgiveness. That's why Jesus's key verse of the Sermon on the Mount is *"Do unto others as you would have them do unto you; this is the Law and the Prophets" (Mathew 7:12).* In this He tells us that this is the meaning of the whole Bible. The rest of the book is just illustration.

Dear friends, you look at trials and temptations as bad things, and yes, bad things happen, and they can change your life forever. But, they are also an opportunity to change and an opportunity to grow. They can change the direction of your life and the life of your children and your children's children. The great thing is that in the trial we can change our direction and our thoughts, and God doesn't hold the past and our past mistakes against us.

That is the wonder and the greatness of God. That *suddenly,* in the blink of an eye, your whole world can be turned around. *God is the master of change.* The point is that God can and does use the trial, the turn in the road, to change you, to call you, and to redirect you forever. God might be leading you today. God might be changing you. Don't turn your back on God's calling, on God's direction, or on God's whispering in your heart.

What is He saying to you today? God is going to use everything—every trial in your life—to His glory. You are wondrously made for His glory and His pleasure. Is it time to turn and see what God has for you and what God wants for you and how God wants to bless you? Every trial that you are going through, everything you have had to go through, is because God wants to use you. It doesn't matter if you are a struggling single mom or that you were an abused child or that you have been in jail or that you were raped or raised in poverty. God can and will use it and you for His glory and your blessing, if you let Him. Today, I can thank God for the struggles, the turns in my life because they have made who I am. Do you see it? Do you see what God might want for you—how God might use the trials in your life to help others and to strengthen you so that you can be the man or woman that God wants you to be? Can you just take a moment to stop and thank God for where you are in your life? See how He is using the trials, the turns, and the pains to produce the praise. Can you believe that?

God uses all your life to bless all of you. When the time is right, God will lead you to the right place. God has a purpose for you and where you are at. Find that purpose and find peace.

Can you *praise Him* right here and now today? If there is anything that will tick off the devil it is that in the midst of your trial, in the midst of your struggles, you are praising God. Can you praise Him? Can you praise and thank Him right now? You might not be in heaven yet, but you can praise Him now. We praise Him in the midst of depression; we praise Him over the trial; and we praise Him through the struggles of life. Paul says in a jail cell, *"I can do all things through Christ who strengthens me."* God will use everything you have been through in your life—good or bad—for His glory. Praise God.

Our text tells us that the kingdom belongs to God. (Kingdom means the domain of the king.) Does He live within your heart, your mind, and your soul? If so, His power and the glory will be with you forever. Amen. Do we really know the God that we serve? Do we really see His power and His glory?

As I stand here, this world is spinning at over one thousand miles per hour. Beyond this, the earth is circling the sun as we travel through the universe. And God holds it all together. He holds the atoms together in the palm of His hand. At His name, demons tremble, and Satan flees. No one can stop Him. No one is His equal. No one is His counselor (even though we try). He lives within the past, the present, and the future. He is here, there, and everywhere all at the same time. He spoke the world and the universe into existence. In the beginning, God created the heavens and the earth, and the earth was formless and void, and He said, "Let there be light, and there was. And it was good, and when He made humankind—when He made you—He said that it was very good. Everything that was created came through Him. He is the Ancient of days. He is the everlasting Father; He is the Prince of Peace, the Alpha and the Omega, the Beginning and the End. He is all knowing (omniscient) and all powerful (omnipotent). He is present here in this room right now, and He is in the depths of the sea. He is here and also at the end of the universe. There is nowhere I can go to hide from Him; there is nowhere to run. He is bigger than any trial I might be facing. He knows every hurt in my life personally. He holds my tears in His bottle.

He is Jehovah, the strong eternal one, He is sovereign; He is the King of Kings and Lord of Lords, Adonai. He is Elohim, the Creator. He is Jehovah-Elyon, the Lord Most High; Jehovah-Jireh, the Lord who provides. He is Jehovah-Mekaddishkem, the Lord our sanctifier; Jehovah-Rapha, the Lord who heals; and Jehovah-Roi, the Lord my shepherd. He is El-Olam, the Everlasting God; El-Shaddai, God Almighty, the nourisher, and the sustainer. His glory is so great that it lights up heaven, so there is no need for a sun. The twenty-four elders fall at His feet and worship. His glory is so great that the angels cover their eyes with wings before Him. Multitudes upon multitudes of angels sing His praise night and day. They sing, "Holy, holy, holy is the Lord God Almighty, the one who was and is and who is to come." The heavens declare His glory. Most of all, He is Jesus, which means, in Hebrew, "the God who saves," and He's my savior and my friend. And He loved me so much that He died for me and for you.

"But made Himself of no reputation taking the form of a bondservant [He emptied himself of all His glory] and coming in the likeness of men. And being found in the appearance of a man He humbled himself and became obedient to the point of death even the death of the cross" (Philippians 2:7–8).

He humbled Himself; He humbled Himself, taking the form of a servant, going to a cross for me. If God is for me, of whom or of what shall I be afraid?

Therefore, don't give up in the storm or the trial. God has a plan for you. He will not give you more than what you can handle—or should I say, what *He* can handle? You might be in a storm, but sooner or later you will get through it; you will come out the other end, and He will never leave you or forsake you. You might be struggling today, but in a few years, you are going to be at another point of your life—another step on the walk of faith. This is all just a part of the process and the leading of the Lord. This too will all pass. Just stay the course; stay on track. Don't give up! Just thank the Lord and don't be afraid. For the person who builds his or her house on the rock (His truth), when the trials and the storms of life come, he or she will not be moved! Remember what Jesus said to Martha when her brother died: *"If you* believe, *you will see the glory of God."*

Glory to God in the highest; glory to God in the highest—amen and amen, so be it. You might be going through a trial, a turn in the road of life, today. You might be facing a cliff. Maybe you have made some mistakes this year, and you have gotten off track. Maybe you are worried about the future. Maybe the devil has got you running scared.

People tell you that you don't have a degree; you don't have money; and you don't have a boyfriend, a husband, or a wife. The devil's got you looking at what you don't have, and you are missing what you do have. Dear friend, it is okay to struggle within life, but it is through your struggle that your cross becomes your crown. It is through the trial that greatness is birthed. If God is closing a door in your life, He will open a window. If He is ending one chapter, get ready for the next one. Maybe something I said has spoken to your heart.

God knows where you are at. He knows if you are lost, and that you need Him. Maybe it is time to get it right with Him. Is it time to look at your life and where you are going and how you are doing and reevaluate? Is what you are doing working? Is it time to make a change—to change the direction you are going?

God humbled Himself unto a cross because He loved you. If you make the choice to serve the Lord, to give your life to Him, you can make it through any storm or any turn in the road. Don't run from the trial, but let the trial run from you. Pray: "Lord, deliver us from evil; deliver us from the evil one." God will take you through the turn, but you need to lean into it.

Wouldn't it be wonderful to know that all the past is forgiven? Wouldn't it be nice to get your life back on track? Know that the Holy Spirit lives within you to give you strength for tomorrow and a new dimension to your life—to give you power and joy and peace that you've never known. He can change your life. It's all yours by giving your life to Christ.

If something I have said has spoken to you, it's the Holy Spirit working, and He is preparing your heart. That little voice inside of you right now is the Holy Spirit trying to get you to come to Christ.

Chapter 4   Self Questions

1. What does it mean to you to be tempted? In what areas of your life are you tempted? How does this relate to your past?

2. What are the major trials in your life?

3. How do you feel about what you have been through?

4. Is the way you feel about these things helpful or hurtful?

5. Why do you think God allows us to go through hard times?

6. What have you learned through your struggles? Is it logical?

7. How do you deal with waiting or dealing with the word *no*?

8. What or who are you committed to in your life?

9. Does your commitment make you happy?

Chapter 4   Homework

Write ten things that you can praise or thank God for.

Chapter 5
CHOOSING TO CHANGE

What do you really want for your life? Is this all there is?
What are you hoping for? Is it to just get by? Or do you want more?
Is this what you were you created for? Is this what God hoped for your life?

Many of us tend to be on this strange roller coaster called life, going around in circles, going nowhere, and for a while, it is fun, but it gets tiring. The question is: Do you want to go around for another ride? Is your life right now what God hoped for when He created you? Do you want to stop the ride and get on with the life that God has for you? Are you willing to get help and deal with the truth your life? Are you willing to step out in faith? Remember: *"Faith is the evidence of things not seen but the substance of things hoped for."* What are you hoping for? Are you waiting on God to do some sort of miracle before you step out of your box? Your life can change. It starts with a choice.

You might be struggling to get by these days, but your future is not defined by your past. It is defined by the choices you make today. There is greatness in you if God is in your heart. God knows your abilities; He has gifted you in a special way for His glory. He has given you the grace for each day. He gives you a future and a hope. It's your choice. Don't be defined by others or by what the world says about you. Don't settle for mediocrity. Realize what God said and what He wants for your life. Or you can stay stuck; you can take another ride on the roller coaster. It's all about your choices.

Paul the apostle prayed that the eyes of your heart (your understanding) would be opened so that you would know the hope of His call and the glory of the inheritance He has for you. Do you know the glory that He has in store for you? He is alive and in you if you have faith in Christ. He has blessed you and will bless you if you let Him. He will even turn your mistakes and failures into blessings if you trust Him.

Again, it's your choice.

Joshua came to the end of his life and gathered the children of Israel together and said these words in Joshua 24:14–15:

> Now, therefore, fear the Lord and serve Him in sincerity and truth, put away the gods which your fathers served beyond the River and in Egypt, and serve the Lord. And if it is disagreeable in your sight to serve the Lord choose for yourselves today whom you will serve.

Joshua was telling the people that they needed to make a choice. All of us need to come to the point of making a choice with our lives and how we are going to live. Real change starts with a decision and a choice.

The prodigal son had to get to the pig pen before he chose to return to the father. He might have been stuck with the pigs, but once he chose to change, he was free—free on the inside. Real power and real change start first in the mind, on the inside—in your heart. God uses the stresses of life to push you to grow and become what He called you to be. What will it take for you to choose to change—to get off the roller coaster? How low do you have to go?

How frustrated do you have to be? Until you make the choice to change, you're going to remain stuck. What will it take for you to make a choice?

God will not force you directly. God respects your right to choose and to follow your will or His. If you want to live your life your way, you can. He will let you find out the truth of your life and the consequences of your own willfulness. But remember this: God is still sovereign. He is still in control; He will have His way in your life. He will get the glory in spite of you and your poor choices. If you are a believer, you are not your own; you were bought with a price. You belong to God. God will let you go to a hell of your own making so that you might call on Him, and that He might save you. That is why He deserves our praise: because He is a God of second and third chances. He is a God who forgives our mistakes and will make them a blessing. He has taken my greatest mistakes and made them into my greatest blessing. Hasn't He blessed you in spite of yourself?

I remember that I used to live in an old step van, like a UPS truck. I would go to parties or friends' houses and get wasted and then go out and sleep in my van. This seemed to work for years, but I got tired of the roller coaster. I got tired of going nowhere with my life. I saw that the drug culture just didn't work—at least not for me. Within a short time, I traded my van for a car that I couldn't sleep in; I got a job and reenrolled in college. I wasn't even a Christian yet, but God was preparing me and molding me to choose Him. I can't say that I stopped using drugs completely, but it wasn't long after that when I stopped for good. *I made that choice of my own free will.*

It is not that different when a person decides to quit smoking; you just get to the point that you say that you are done. If you don't choose it, you will just go around again on that roller coaster. Too many people don't really make the choice.

Many times the motivation is that you want something more. You want a new life, but you're afraid. How many people quit smoking when their doctor tells them that they have cancer? How many people choose to lose weight when they get divorced? What will it take for you to come to the point of making the choice to change your life? You don't have to get to the pigsty to change. Some people call this hitting bottom; some people see it as surrendering to God. It is when you realize that Christ is the only answer. The point is you have to make that choice and stop blaming the world or circumstances for you being miserable. In the end, your life is not where you are now but where you are going. Do you know where you are going and who is going to get you there? It's your choice. I find that too many people are stuck in self-pity. Too many people are blaming others, so they don't make the choice to change. Your destiny is in your next choice, your next decision. You say that it is up to God; God says that it is up to you. We look to God for change; God is looking to you. If you do what you always do, you will be where you always have been. It is up to you.

Controlling Fear

The truth is: if you don't control your fears, your fears will control you.

What stops us from being all that we hope to be? What stops us from stepping into a new life—the new life that God promised? Fear! Are we afraid to let go of the old life we are used to for the future we don't know or trust God for? God works in the world of the supernatural—the unbelievable—and it scares us. He asks us to step out of the boat and onto the water. He calls us to march around the walls of Jericho and watch it fall; He tells us to feed the crowd with a few loaves and fish. Will we believe? Will we trust Him? The opposite of faith is fear, not unbelief.

What keeps a person from leaving an abusive relationship? Fear! The fear of admitting that you made a mistake, the fear of being alone, the fear that believes that you will never be loved, or the fear of rejection.

A man has a heart attack and then bypass surgery, and, from fear, he suddenly begins to eat right, exercise, and do the things the doctor tells him. He might even quit smoking. After some months or a year goes by and the fear dissipates, he forgets about the possibility of death. Denial sets in, and he is back to his old ways.

Is fear controlling you? Is it stopping you from the blessing that God wants for you? Are you afraid of what you might lose if you choose to serve the Lord? Joshua said to *put away the gods of Egypt,* the old lifestyle. Maybe you need to walk away from things or people that you thought you had to have. You have to let go of the old wants, loves, and hates to get the blessing. I really did love using drugs and that lifestyle, but I loved God more. Do you love God more than the things or persons that keep you from Him? Or are you afraid to let them go?

Are you afraid to try something new or to think about things in a new way? You might be one new thought away from a breakthrough, from a new life, and from a new beginning. Are you just afraid to step out in faith and trust God or trust anyone? I find that people will not choose to change unless they are more afraid of what might or will happen if they don't.

The Bible states: "Perfect love cast out fear." God's love for us and our faith in Him is greater than fear. This is the victory that overcomes the world (overcomes our fears): our faith. It is a faith in one thing, one person—the Lord Jesus Christ—that overcomes fear. It is faith that gives us hope for a new life. Our faith is in the victor, who is Christ, and in no one else. Is your love for Him greater than your fears—greater than your love for the world? Is He your prize and hope? Do you know His power and His presence? Do you trust Him more than you trust yourself? He has promised to bless you if you trust Him. Do you believe it? His power is here. He will be with you.

But didn't Joshua say that we should fear the Lord? What does that mean?

When we are controlled by our own wants, needs, and fears we miss the mark: we sin. *We miss the blessing that God wants for our lives.* Too often I find that people play with God. They have faith when it is convenient, but God has a way of getting their attention.

My Father never really confronted his life or faith until he faced cancer. It seems that many of us have to go through hell to call out for heaven. Jonah didn't call to God until he was in the belly of the fish. What will it take for us to stop making excuses? How might God confront our pride, our attitude, our arrogance—personally or as a nation? The truth is that I am afraid. I don't mess with God; there are some games I just don't want to play. I know what it is like when God puts on the pressure or squeezes you to choose and repent and change the direction of your life. God let me go through the hell of my own making, but He lifted me up when I called to Him. How many of you have had to go through hell to get on your knees? Or is your life hell right now?

Joshua 24:14 says, *"Now therefore fear the Lord and serve Him in sincerity."*

Paul tells us in Philippians 2:12, *"Work out our salvation with fear and trembling."*

Psalm 2:11 states, *"Worship the Lord with reverence, and rejoice with trembling."*

To be honest, that sounds a little strange.

What is this all about? How can we love someone we fear? Yes, the idea relates to respect. I think the idea is more that we need to live our lives with an eye toward heaven, realizing that God is still in control, that God is still God, and that He sees all. You can't just fake it to make it. With real faith comes real sacrifice of self. Jesus left His glory in heaven for a greater glory. He sacrificed Himself that we might pick up our cross and follow Him. Do you really know

Him? Does it scare you that you might gain the world but lose your soul? God is not mocked; we reap what we sow, or as they say on the street, what goes around comes around. Is this all true? If it is, how should we live our lives with respect to God or in respect to how we treat others? What does it really mean to love Him?

Until you take your faith to the place of all your hurts and fears, you will never know the blessing and love that God has for you. God has given you the potential to live a life that is beyond your fears—until you choose to change, to let go of the past, to give your life to Christ and His authority, and until you choose to trust Him alone. You will waste your life going in circles. Are you just wasting time? Choose to praise Him, choose to trust Him, and choose to serve Him.

Beware of Victimization

Many people sabotage their lives by seeing themselves as victims of life. If all we see is the possibility of hurt or failure, the more fear controls us. We lose the joy of life the more we become bitter and frustrated. Like some evil tape that runs through our thinking, it controls us. We victimize ourselves. We hear the words we were told growing up: "You're no good; you will never be successful."

Recognize that all negative thoughts are not true; don't let them define you. Don't let them become your reality. It is your choice. You are not defined by your past hurt or where you are from or what your family said about you. You can make a choice for a new life. If you focus on wrong or negative things, you give those thoughts power in your life. They rob your joy and peace. Remember the truth that God loves you, and He has your back; He has a purpose for your life. Your thoughts and your choices will make you or break you. The power is in your hands, in your thoughts, and in your choice. Don't be afraid of the opportunities, the potential, or the future that God provides. He has the ability to open a window when a door is shut, the ability to make a way, and the ability to take away fear because He loves you. Will you trust Him for your tomorrow? The hard times are an opportunity to look at things in a new light and make new choices for the future.

David said in Psalm 27:1: *"The Lord is my light and my salvation; Whom shall I fear? The Lord is the strength of my life; of whom shall I be afraid?"*

Seeing yourself as a victim sets you up for failure. Not only this, but if you see yourself as a victim, you can justify any action. An example would be that if you see yourself being stuck in poverty, as a victim of the system, you might justify stealing, lying, etc. to get what you want. Why? Because that is the only way you feel that you can get what you think you need. The truth is, *life isn't fair,* but that is *no excuse.* Too often, when you feel that you have no control over your life, your failures will become excuses to blame everyone else.

For some, when life gets tough, they stop trying, or they quit. The truth is that life is hard, and it's a struggle for all of us. Don't wait on the world to change to get on with your life. Maybe God is waiting on you to change or for you to make a choice so that He might bless you. Do you have the courage and the faith to choose a new life?

It is *the optimist* who sees that he or she has control over his or her life. That truth pushes that person to work harder to get what he or she wants, and that person generally gets it. It is *the pessimist* who says, "I can never win." So why try? Why keep pushing? That doesn't mean ignoring the past or the hurts or the losses of the past, but it does mean not being stuck in the past. It's mourning and accepting losses and moving on.

Let's face it, just about everyone who has accomplished great things has had to overcome difficulties. Even if you were born with all the advantages of life, there will be times that you will get a raw deal or a bad hand dealt to you. The question really is: How will you play the cards that you have been dealt?

Everyone who plays poker will get a bad hand dealt to them sometimes, but a good poker player knows that it is all in *how you play the hand.*

This is all easier said than done, but it leads me to the question: What do you want? Is this where you want to be in your life? You have the power to change your circumstances. You have the power to make the choice. Do you really believe that? As long as you see yourself as the victim, you will stay stuck. The time to make your move is now. The time for change, the time for a new life, begins with a choice. You are more than your past; you are more than where you are from. It is about where you are going. It's about your future, and it's about your choice. You are one choice from losing weight, ending drug use, or leaving an abusive relationship. You are one choice from making a new reality.

The trick to all this begins by taking responsibility for where you are at in your life. It takes courage, knowledge, and insight to look at yourself and ask the question: "Who am I?" Is this what I want to be? You must choose to do it. No one can do it for you.

One time in counseling, a young person gave me a great thought. Even though he was struggling, my guess was that he had been to too many counselors before he spoke with me. Commenting on his life, he said these insightful words: "If you have one foot standing in the past and one foot in the future, all you are doing is crapping on today." In other words if you focus your thoughts on the past or if you worry about the future too much, all you do is mess up today. Where are you stuck in your life? Do your past hurts, your failures, and your fear of future pain dominate your thinking? Is it robbing your joy? It is important to gain insight into what you have done and ask yourself if you are still making the same mistakes over and over. Then it is time to come up with a new plan for dealing with your life.

Take a moment to look at your life and ask yourself what things you wish you could have done better. Maybe you could have made better choices in relationships, in careers, or in goals for your life. Maybe you could have treated people better. Does what you do end up hurting you or others? God can forgive you of those past mistakes. You can make it right. It is your choice.

The question is: *"Are you making the same types of mistakes today?"* If so, what will happen if you continue along this path? Is that what you want for yourself?

Now comes the defining moment. If you are not happy with the way things are, what bad choices or patterns of behavior do you need to get rid of? What, then, do you want to change? A choice, a premise, or a new thought can make all the difference. A choice opens everything to a new potential and a changed future.

I like what Joshua tells the children of Israel. He tells them to look and see what God has done in the past for them before they make their choice. Joshua retells all the wonders of leaving Egypt and God's provision. Are there any things you might be thankful to God for? Has He helped you in the past? Can you list the things that you are thankful to Him for? Will that help you in trusting Him for the future?

Remember when you asked God to get you out of a situation, or you felt as if you were drowning in life's problems, and God pulled you out of it. Remember the times you struggled to make ends meet; you didn't know how you were going to feed yourself and your children with so little, but somehow food showed up. God brought you through it. Remember your child being sick, and you prayed, "Lord, help me," and He did. Remember that relationship you asked God to heal and He didn't, and now you are thankful. Remember the times you cried into the night and you thought the heartache wouldn't stop. Your thoughts of him or her or of some trauma would not get out of your head. But you made it through, and with God's help, you are here, still standing. Dear friend, *the hardest lesson in life is when God asks us to trust Him.*

This just might be a defining moment of your life. God has brought you to this place where you are because He wants you to take stock of your life. He wants to move you to a new level of faith. Is it time to make a choice? Is it time to let go of the past and step into your new future? Have you wasted too many years being stuck or going in circles?

The Bible talks about repentance. But what does that mean? It means to turn around and change direction in your life. It means making a new choice for your life. It means acknowledging to God where or how you have messed up and taking responsibly for your part. It is acknowledging that you want something better. It is knowing that God has something better in store for you. It is saying to God that you are *willing* to do things His way. You don't have to be perfect; God will help you to change if you are truly willing.

It is realizing that *"I can do all things through Christ who strengthens me."*

It is an act of the will. It's a choice! It's *your choice*! It is a choice to do your best to serve and obey Him. It is realizing that you are not home yet but on a step along the way. It is believing that God has a future prepared for you. It is choosing to live out what you were created for, praising Him. In that praise, the real joy in life is found. It is knowing that everything that you have been through in this life will work for His glory. It's about choosing and trusting Christ over self.

It doesn't matter if you are rich or if you are poor. You can be a member of a church or born into a Christian family, but you need to choose to let your new life begin.

Do you feel that you need to make a change? Make a new choice to serve and praise the Lord. Can you truly commit to a new lifestyle, a new way of thinking, and a new way of living? God can help you in the areas that you are stuck, if you are honest with Him and with yourself.

5 Self Questions

1. Do you control your life, or does life (drug abuse, anger, circumstances) control you? Why or why not?

2. What areas of your life are you afraid to talk about or hurt too much to talk about?

3. Are you living up to what you want for your life? Are you living to what God would like for your life? What areas might need an adjustment?

4. Are you living up to what those who love you want for you?

5. What would they say to you?

6. Who are you? Is this the reputation that you want for your life?

7. Does what you do hurt yourself and others?

8. Do you see yourself as a victim or a victor in life—a pessimist or an optimist?

9. Who do you blame from the past for where you are in your life? What is your biggest fear for the future? Does this affect your life today?

10. Do you want to change? What will happen if you don't change?

11. To choose something new, you have to let go of something old. What are you afraid to let go of?

12. What will happen if you don't let it go?

13. Are you willing to come to Christ? Do you really feel that you can trust Him for your future?

Chapter 5   Homework

1. Write down the things that you wish you could have done better.

2. List how you are making the same mistakes today.

3. List the bad things that you need to exchange for the good.

4. Where will you be in five years if you don't choose to change? Is that what you want?

Chapter 6

MOVING FORWARD

Philippians 3:12–14:

> *Not that I have already obtained it, or have already become perfect,*
> *but I press on in order that I may lay hold of that, for which also I was*
> *laid hold of by Christ Jesus. Brethren, I do not regard myself as having*
> *laid hold of it yet; but one thing I do: forgetting what lies behind and*
> *reaching forward to what lies ahead I press on toward the goal for the*
> *price of the upward call of God in Christ Jesus.*

Shakespeare told us, "All's well that ends well." It's not how you start the race, it's how you finish. It's not how you start the job, the marriage, your life, but how it ends. Ending well is important. Now you might be discouraged at this point in your life, but this is just a step along the way. God will use all of your life, even your struggles, for His purpose. The truth is that if you choose to follow Christ, He is going to change you and mold you into His image. He will allow circumstances to get you to pray to change. Remember, prayer changes you, not God. Through your struggles and through those times on your knees, you find your purpose; you find peace; you find direction. The point is that your life means something. Your life matters to eternity. Your life and your relationship with God matters. It's not what you are going through or have gone through it, it is that God loves you and is with you. The Bible teaches that as a believer, you are in a process. You are not home yet; your life isn't over; you haven't reached God's goal, the prize that He has for you.

Do you have a plan for your life, or do you take life as it comes? Are you making it up as you go along? God has a purpose and a schedule for your life. In His time, God is changing you and growing you to become more like Christ and to have Christ live in you. The goal is Christ! The purpose of Christianity is to be like Christ. Paul, in fact, says, *"To live is Christ."* What or who are you living for? Do you see God's guidance and His hand in your life? Can you thank Him for where you are at and how you got here? Does something need to change?

In the text, Paul is saying that in spite of his circumstances, he is still striving to run the race of faith—to know Christ, His power, and His presence in his life. He is saying that even though he is facing death, he is not done; he is not quitting. Paul might be in a jail cell, but his soul (his spirit) is free. He sees God's hand where he is at. When you know that where you are at and what you have been through is being used for God's plan and purpose, it invigorates you to not give up. When you understand that your struggles, your sufferings, are no greater than Christ's, it binds you to Him; it changes your perspective. *It's knowing that God hurt just like you.* That changes you. It empowers you. It's knowing that He hurts with you because He is with you. It's knowing that He really hears you. It's knowing: *"I can do all things through Christ who strengthen me."* Where you are right now in your life is important to God; you are right where you are supposed to be. So don't give up. Keep on believing, even if you lose your house, your job, or your health. Be faithful in the little things, and God will give you more. Don't give up hope. This might just be the moment that God wants to change you to take you to a higher level of faith.

God knows where you are at, and He will be with you and use it all for His glory. I believe that no matter what you are dealing with God, wants to and will bless you through it. Just remember: *"The battle belongs to the Lord."* He will win;

in the end, He will get the glory. Therefore, Paul, in spite of his circumstances, tells us in the book of Philippians *"to press on…to rejoice always…to be anxious for nothing…to pray…to be thankful…to think about what is pure, right…, and praiseworthy."* These are the things that guard our hearts and minds; these are the things that give peace and hope. Paul concludes with this truth: *"I can do all things through Christ who strengthens me" (Philippians 4:13).*

Too many of us are like the children of Israel, wandering in the desert, going in circles.

The question is: Do you really want to get to the promised land? Are there areas in your life that need to change? Do you know the thoughts and actions that keep you in your frustration? Are you tired of the desert of your life? Maybe this is the time and the place where God is going to open things up for you. God wants to restore your life.

Until we step out in faith, until we trust God for our future, new life won't happen. Until we confront our past hurts, pains, *and fears that keep us from faith and hope,* change won't come. God doesn't want us to become more religious or to follow more rules. He wants a real relationship with us. God will give us the grace and power to do it. Will we look at our lives from God's perspective and potential? Do we want more of Christ? Do we see what God might be teaching us or calling us to confront within ourselves? Do we see the things that we do or the things that control us that rob our blessings? Do we really want to know Him and the power of His resurrection?

The problem with most of us is that it is hard to admit our weakness and our need. Especially for church people, it is hard to admit when we are overwhelmed or when we feel that God isn't listening. Can we bring our hurt and our real lives to God? Can we really pray for each other about the things that hurt? Is it hard to admit that we need to change?

What areas do you *feel that you need to change? What might God be telling you to change? What is stopping you from living completely for Christ? Is it anger? Is it fear? Is it an addiction or compulsion?* I might be able to tell you what areas you might need to change, but for the change to take place you need to take responsibility and come up with a plan that you can own.

Maybe it would be a good idea to pray and ask the Lord what areas you need to work on. If that doesn't work, ask your spouse or your family. They just might be the voice you need to hear.

Looking at your life, if you could change anything about yourself, what would that be? In what areas would you like to grow? Where might God be prompting you to change? What would it take to have a better relationship with Christ?

Take a moment and look at the areas of your life. What are the areas where Christ doesn't rule? What are you struggling with today? What sin keeps you from God? What are areas of your life that you are afraid to bring to God? What is holding you down? Where might God be testing you to trust Him today?

- **Your Relationships, Family**
  Are your relationships keeping you from Christ? Do you listen to the wrong people and the wrong voices? Does what others think about you or say about you control you? Do your family or friend relationships poison your life?

- **Your Work or School**
  Does want you do or what you are being taught lead you away from God?

- **Your Physical Health**

  Are you afraid to confront your medical issues because you're afraid that the truth might hurt? Why don't you take care of the body the Lord has given you? Does it fill you with worry?

- **Your Spiritual Needs**

  Is the Lord the first thing you think about in the morning and the last thing at night? Do you miss the Lord when you don't read His word or fellowship with believers?

- **Your Character/Honesty, Values, and Reputation**

  Is what people see what they get? Are you real? Can people believe what they see? Do you have integrity? Do you have character, or are you just a character?

- **Your Emotions, Anger, Depression, Fear**

  Do your emotions and past get the better of you? Do things like anger, bitterness, and pride run your life? Are you discouraged with life? Does life seem to always get worse?

- **Substance Abuse, Drug or Alcohol use, Tobacco, Overeating, Finances, Gambling, Relationships, etc.**

  Do your vices stop you from experiencing the life that God wants for you? What comes before your relationship with Christ? Where or with what do you spend most of your money or time?

Do you love God more than all of these things? Is your relationship with God worth more to you than your wants and needs? Is God putting you in a situation where you have to trust Him? Where do you need to grow in your faith? Where do you need to pick up your cross and follow Him? Where do you have to stand alone with God? What gets between you and God? Is God pressing you in any of these areas?

Do you believe that you can deal with all of these things through Christ? Jesus wants to touch you; Jesus wants to help you. Jesus wants to set you free. Do you have the faith to trust him and to let Him help with your problems? Are you willing to change? Do you know that you have the grace to deal with life? Doing nothing changes nothing; only when we step out in faith do things change. Of these areas, where do you need to change?

Paul said, *"This one thing I do is press on."* Are you pressing on? Where do you need to grow? Is there something within your spirit that you know needs to change? What is blocking your relationship with God or with those you love? Ask God to reveal it to you. Faith comes from hearing and hearing from the Word of God. What is His word saying to you? Where is your faith? The truth is that if you don't deal with your life, you will stay in the desert. You will miss the blessing Have you learned the secret?

"I can do all things through Christ who strengthens me" (Philippians 4:13).

God is changing you! Trust Him. Praise Him.

"Eyes have not seen, ears have not heard what the Lord has prepared for those who love Him" (1 Corinthians 2:9).

As I look at my life, the thing that kept me from Christ—that kept me from really living—was *fear and insecurity.* It was the fear of rejection, the fear of failure, that drove me to become the person that I am today. I realize that I grew up in a family in which no matter what I did, I could not please my father. That led me to try to please others with my life. Maybe my insecurity came from the fact that I couldn't remember my father ever saying that he loved me. It is because of this hole within me that I work hard to do things right or know all the facts in order to get acceptance. Generally, *we all want love and acceptance.* Don't you? But Christ loves me and accepted me just as I am.

The point here is for you to come up with the answers to these questions. You probably know the answers within yourself already. You know what really hurts in your life; you know what your real struggles are. You know what you really need to change! The question now becomes: What do you want to do about it? There is a way to fix this. What would you have to do to let God heal your life? I can't tell you the answer. That is for you to figure out. You need to process this for yourself. You need to come up with a plan.

Here are some questions that you might want to ask yourself:

- How must I trust God to fix this?
- What needs to change?
- If I had a magic wand, what would I do?
- What does God really want me to do?
- How might I be responsible for where I am at?
- How might I not be responsible? What was beyond my control?
- Do I really believe that God is able?
- If I were God, I would _____.
- What do I or we need to do to move forward?
- What would I tell someone if they came to me for advice about this?
- If I don't change or come up with a plan to deal with my issues, what is going to happen in the future?

In Philippians 4, Paul again shares how he weeps for the future of those who will not make changes. He goes on to say in verse 19, "*Whose end is destruction, whose god is their appetite, and whose glory is in their shame....*" Their god is self.

I, too, look at the lives of so many people, and it is as if a train wreck is going to happen if they continue doing what they are doing. And they just do not see it, or they won't see it. But in the end, *the truth will always come to the light.* For some people, life is good no matter who they hurt or what they do. Worse still, it seems that they think that what they are doing is fine. *But do not be deceived, God is not mocked; we will reap what we sow (Galatians 5:7).*

We live in world where we want all the credit, but we blame others when things go wrong. Isn't that what our political leaders do? We live for the moment and do not think much about tomorrow. We hear, "Have a good time; party; don't worry." We escape in our addictions and entertainment. It seems that we are so full of ourselves that we don't want to admit that we need to change. Is this a type of selfish pride and narcissism, where we say we don't need God or others, where we just want to do things our way? Is it self-righteousness and pride? Some people say that we are going to hell in a hand basket, but at least we feel good about it.

Don't let pride rob your blessings, joy, and peace. Let God set you free from the things that control your life. Do it for yourself. It cost Him too much for you to stay stuck. It cost Him too much for you to let circumstances, addiction, anger, fear, and bitterness control your life. A little faith can move mountains in your life. Our *"faith is the victory that has overcome the world"* (1 John 5:4).

Isn't it time for you to start taking ownership of your life? That takes courage, facing what frightens you the most. That means letting go of one reality for another. It means being totally honest with yourself. It is being able to admit to yourself and to someone else the worst thing that you have ever done to another person. It is admitting where you have failed. It is realizing how you have hurt yourself and the people you love or sometimes realizing that the people who are supposed to love you, didn't or don't know how. It is seeing that you might have to let go of something old before you get something new.

Options

The question now becomes: What do you want to do about it? Will you step out in faith? What could you try to do to make things better or to make things right in your life? Does it mean going to a class or getting counseling or dropping certain people in your life? Does it mean setting boundaries with some people—maybe your own children? Does it mean changing your lifestyle or even your beliefs about reality or yourself? What do you want to work on? What do you want to change? You might want to think about it like this: What would someone you know who loves you tell you to do (even someone who has passed away)? If you can't think of anyone who has ever loved you, what would God tell you to do?

Find Support

The Bible says: *seek and you will find, ask and you will receive, knock and the door will be opened unto you.* My point is that you need to find some support. Find a group or find people who will give you honest feedback as you move forward. These are the types of people who are not afraid to tell you when you are wrong or going off your plan.

I don't mean just critical people; I mean people you know who really want the best for you. *One of the keys in life is finding those people who care about and want the best for you and staying away from those who don't.* These are people who might hold you accountable to yourself and to your dreams and plan with you and support you along the way to reach and accomplish your goals. They are people who love you too much to see you fail.

Too often we go to critical people to get support, and all we get is criticized. *People can't give you what they don't have.* We can't get answers from people who don't know or who haven't experienced it. It is like the blind leading the blind. You need to find the right friends and the right teachers if you want to go the right direction. I might not have had the best father to guide me, but I found men that I admired and looked up to who showed me the way. I personally want to thank the Rev. Dr. Ralph Didier for being a role model through the years. He taught me what it meant to be a man of God. Surround yourself with the right people: the people who have been where you are at and who have gone to where you want to be. They can show you the way. If you can't find any of them around, look to books, DVDs, or the teachings of people who are on the path of who you want to be. There are also counselors, life coaches, or groups that might help you.

This is for you: Do you need make a commitment to yourself to change? Are you ready to live your life on purpose? Also know this: God has, and will, provided people in your life to show you the way—people who have been there and done it. If you open your eyes, you can get direction, glean truth, and find hope. The trick is in knowing who to listen to and knowing who really has your back. Look to see if their actions match their words. It's about being discerning.

Find people in your life who have overcome what you are trying to master. You are who you hang with. If you hang out with millionaires, soon you might become one as well. It might sound far-fetched, but there is the truth that people become like who they follow or admire. If you can't find people, find books where people have overcome a similar issue. See how God will use it and you for his Glory. Remember that His hand is on you.

You might be going through hard times. Let me tell you that those hard times will tell you who really cares, who really has your back, and who really loves you. God has a plan for your life. He will provide a way, whether it's a job, a family, a friend, or a helping hand. No matter what, God is still God, and He is in control, in spite of seemingly insurmountable setbacks or failures. We just don't see it. But Paul, sitting in a jail cell, understood. Paul knew that in due time, *"Every knee shall bow and every tongue will confess that Jesus Christ is Lord...for it is God who works in you both to will and to do, for His good pleasure" (Philippians 2:10–13).*

I challenge you to write down your options; change your focus from what is going wrong to what is right. Paul tells you to let your mind dwell on the good things. Write down the things that you are thankful for; write your goals and plans to move yourself forward. Talk to a friend and supportive family members about your plans. Ask them for not just advice but what they think about your plan. Does it really make sense to them? Pray about it; does what you hope for fit with the Word of God?

Once you have come up with a plan and have written it down, if you have to, look at it every day to keep your mind focused on what you want for yourself, what you want to change, and what you want to do. I remember writing my goals and thoughts on 3 by 5 cards and reading them daily until they became a part of my thinking. As you move along this process, check to see if what you are doing is working. If not, try something else, but don't be afraid to make some mistakes along the way. Be faithful in the little things and see where God opens doors or situations. Don't be afraid to work hard. Follow the blessings; look for His providence and His favor. Nothing just happens in our lives; look for the purpose. God has a plan for you. He has a future and a hope for you. Will you trust Him?

Your life is not a mistake. Remember, you can use everything you are going through or have gone through as an opportunity to help others. You just might be the voice or the hand that someone else needs. In being a blessing to others, you are blessed. You are never too young or too old or too poor to be a blessing.

If things are working well, give yourself little rewards for meeting your goals. Notice the positive steps that you are taking. Praise and thank Him along the way. God will remember your faithfulness. He wants to bless you; He loves you. All things work for the good in His time. Your life isn't over until God says it is over. So don't give up.

Remember that some issues stay with us for a lifetime. Yes, you can make situations better, but the memory is still there, though it doesn't have to control you. You can learn to look at it with a new perspective. I have been away from drugs for some thirty years, but the other day someone showed me some new medical marijuana, and I thought that maybe just one puff for "scientific" purposes wouldn't hurt. I didn't do it, but that thought was still there. Remember that we all get dumb, negative thoughts at times. Just realize what they are: *dumb thoughts!*

Work on one issue at a time. Don't bite off more than you can chew. How do you eat an elephant? One bite at a time. What *one* thing is important to you to change? Dealing with too much at one time will frustrate you and make you want to give up. I have heard it said that if you work on one seemingly small change for yourself, to others it will look like a big change. You just don't see it. You don't have to be perfect; take things in small steps. Remember, Jesus told us to be faithful in the little things. If we are faithful in the little, He will give us more. Zechariah 4:10 says,

> *"Do not despise these small beginnings, for the Lord rejoices to see the work begin...."*

Let's say that your issue relates to your temper. Instead of going from zero to ten quickly in your anger, work on just going to five. Tell yourself things like, "I wish that she or he weren't like that, but I understand that he or she is doing the best that person can do. I don't have to take it personally." It is realizing that hurting people hurt people. My point is to take things in small steps. The real issue is not giving up on yourself; you can do it! It was Churchill who said, *"Success is moving from one failure to another with enthusiasm."* Don't quit; don't give up on yourself. Realize that you are just in a process of changing—a step along the way. Remember that we walk and live by faith one step at a time. It is a process. Trust in the Lord. Know that God has something better for you.

One thing to remember in the entire struggle are the words of Paul from Philippians 1:6:

"For I am confident of this very thing, that He who began a good work in you will complete it...."

Chapter 6   Self Questions

Which of these areas would you like to work on first? Pick one and develop a plan. Read that section of the chapter daily.

- Your Relationships with Family or Friends
- Your Work or School
- Your Physical Health
- Your Spiritual Needs
- Your Character/Honesty, Values, and Reputation
- Your Emotions, like Anger, Depression, Fear, etc.
- Substance Abuse, Drug or Alcohol use, Tobacco, Overeating, Finances, Gambling, etc.
- Other

1. If you were to die tonight, what goals or dreams would you miss out on? What area do you want to work on today? (Note the areas listed above.)

2. What do you want to do about the area that you want to change? If you had magic or if you were "Superman," what would you do?

3. Is there a way to fix it? What is it? When will you do it? Is there someone who might hold you accountable to help you complete your goal? Who?

4. What would happen if you don't change it?

5. What scares you about changing?

6. What old view or goal might you have to exchange for this new one?

Chapter 6   Homework

Write down your options for dealing with your chosen issue.

After writing your goals, look at them daily.

Write what someone who loves you would tell you to do.

Find a support group.

Write down where you might go to find people who have dealt with a similar issue.

Chapter 7

DEALING WITH FALSE EXPECTATIONS AND DEPRESSION

Have you ever felt that your hopes and dreams were not coming to pass? Have you ever felt like giving up? Have you ever felt all alone like no one cares, not even God? I have. Have you ever prayed for a person or something, and it seemed that no one was listening? I have. Have you ever expected your life to go one way, and it didn't?

Let me say this: Paul prayed for healing three times, and it didn't come. Three times the apostle called on the Lord, and there was no healing. But the Lord said to him, *"My grace is enough; my grace is sufficient…strength is perfected in weakness."*

That night in the garden, Jesus struggled within His soul to the point of death and asked the disciples three times to pray for Him, and they fell asleep. He asked His Father to take the cup (the trial: the cross) from Him. But Jesus said, "Your will be done." Have you struggled within your soul to accept His will for your life?

We live in a world that expects to buy its way out of every problem. We seem to think that we can control, legislate, or buy our way out of every tough situation. That is a lie. We falsely believe that life revolves around us, but life isn't about us; it's about God. The hardest lesson that He has taught me in the dark times was to *trust Him.* The problem is *expectations.* We have churches that teach that we all should be rich or that we all should be healed if we just had the faith. But everyone isn't healed, and everyone isn't rich. Can you say to God, "Your grace is enough"? Can you say, "Your will be done on earth as it is in heaven"?

Until we stop putting our own agenda on God, we will never have peace. Until we stop putting our expectations upon the Lord, we will not hear His voice or know His presence. God has made you who you are and has given you the grace to deal with your life. He has given you the power to live life abundantly. Jesus said, "Peace I give unto you, not as the world gives." But you need to give your whole self to Him. You need to trust Him with all your heart, mind, soul, and strength.

Jesus said, "Come unto me and I will give you rest; I will give you peace." Do you know His peace? Do you know that rest? Sometimes I think that we all struggle in trusting the Lord.

Elijah was a man of God who called down fire from heaven, prayed for the rain to come, and rejoiced when it came. He raised a boy from the dead and had a showdown with 450 prophets of Baal and won. He was the "man." But after things didn't go as he expected, Elijah was threatened by Jezebel, filled with fear, and ran off into the desert and hoped to die. He forgot God's truth; he forgot God's presence, and he thought he was alone. Do you feel alone today? Is the stress of life robbing your joy?

1 Kings 19:1ff:

¹Now Ahab told Jezebel everything Elijah had done and how he had killed all the prophets with the sword. ² So Jezebel sent a messenger to

Elijah to say, "May the gods deal with me, be it ever so severely, if by this time tomorrow I do not make your life like that of one of them."

[3] Elijah was afraid[a] (if there is one thing that will destroy your life and control you, it is FEAR, fear of life, fear of failure, fear for tomorrow, even the fear of being afraid) and ran for his life. When he came to Beersheba in Judah, he left his servant there, [4] while he himself went a day's journey into the wilderness. (He was physically and emotionally tired, empty and alone) He came to a broom bush, (a juniper tree, maybe he was looking for water) sat down under it and prayed that he might die. "I have had enough, Lord," he said. (Have you ever felt like that?) "Take my life; I am no better than my ancestors." [5] Then he lay down under the bush and fell asleep. (Never choose a long term solution i.e. death, quitting on life, for a short term problem, a threat, or a fear, especially when you are tired and exhausted.)

All at once an angel touched him and said, "Get up and eat." [6] He looked around, and there by his head was some bread baked over hot coals, and a jar of water. He ate and drank and then lay down again.

[7] The angel of the Lord came back a second time and touched him and said, "Get up and eat, for the journey is too much for you." [8] So he got up and ate and drank. Strengthened by that food, he traveled forty days and forty nights until he reached Horeb, the mountain of God. [9] There he went into a cave and spent the night.

Is there someone reading this who is ready to give up? You want to quit; you want to run away? Tired of a marriage, tired of the kids, tired of the job, or an uncaring boss? Tired of church, tired of life?

There were times in my life when I felt like Elijah—when I just wanted to run away from it all. I was in my thirties when my father died at sixty from a strange brain cancer; maybe it was from working with the navy and watching an atomic bomb go off. They told him that the sunglasses would protect him; my mother died the year before my father, after nine months in intensive care. I got the bill back in 1988, and it was for $1.5 million. She had suffered a stroke that left her speechless and paralyzed, and then they found cancer. To top it off, from all the drugs they gave her to keep her alive, her kidneys were destroyed, and she had to be on dialysis daily. And because of fear, I could not stay in the room and watch her die, which will be an everlasting shame in my life. I asked the doctors to stop dialysis, but I couldn't watch her die. I didn't want to face that truth. And these were just half of the issues that I was confronting at the time. And I prayed, and I prayed, and it seemed like I was alone. I just didn't know how God was working it all for my good at the time. Like Elijah, for a moment I thought that I was alone, but God never left me or forsook me. I just didn't see how He was working it for the good. I felt like Job. But Job had faith because he says, "There is hope for a tree, if it be cut down, that it will sprout again, and that its shoots will not cease." He was right: through all my losses, I have been doubly blessed.

Elijah was at the top of his game; he had beaten the enemy and had called down the fire and the rain. But He was tired, and he lost hope; and when you lose hope, you lose faith.

Hebrews 11 says, *"Now faith is the substance of things hoped for, the evidence of things not seen."*

Why might you feel broken and depressed? Have you lost your hope?

I was speaking with a Christian woman who was struggling to hold back the tears. She told me that her husband filed for divorce no real reason after twenty-nine years of marriage. She was a woman of faith, but she lost hope; her life wasn't going as she had expected or wanted. She didn't want a divorce, but she blamed herself. Have you ever been there? I tried to show her that her life was not over, and that God still had a plan for her. In fact, I knew that God was going to bless her.

Elijah lost hope. He expected God to do one thing, and He didn't. Maybe he thought that the people would repent and come back to the Lord, after seeing God send the fire from heaven. One of the biggest disappointments in life is when things don't go as you plan. You pray for the right man or woman to come into your life; you find him or her and have a big wedding, and suddenly, after three months, you realize that person is not the person you thought he or she would be. You pray to the Lord for a child or grandchild to fill your life with joy, and that child is born with Down syndrome or develops cancer, and your world is turned upside down. You expected happily ever after, and it didn't happen. It is even worse if you are a Christian because you know that God has all this power, and it seems that He doesn't help you or use it for you. It seems that God is against you. And you come to church, and people ask you how you are doing, and all you can say is, "Fine." Because that is what you are supposed to say. Do you know what I am talking about?

We can never know all the whys in this life, God's ways are not our ways, and we are not His counselor. Life is not fair, but God is, and He will help you get through it.

Let me stop and say something about feelings. *Feelings* are not right or wrong, they just are. Most of the time feelings are just reflections of our past, good or bad. They affect the way we think about things and life, and they can lie to us, and we believe the lies. Remember, who is the father of lies? Satan wants to mess with your head. You might be a beautiful woman, but you feel ugly because you remember being laughed at or being called ugly as a kid. Or maybe you were made to feel stupid by what others said. But it isn't true. Those false feelings and thoughts affect you today. Those lies you believe about yourself affect you today. As I have a said before, *"It is easier to believe a lie than deal with the truth." We deny truth.* How many of us have believed lies about ourselves? What others have said: "You're going to be loser like your father." *"You can never change."* I think people have a hard time being honest with themselves, their life, their flaws, and their family. Realize this, dear friend. For most of us, there is a hole in our lives that only Christ can fill. We try to fill it with drugs, things, relationships, money, etc., and it just doesn't work. Only Christ can truly meet our needs and fill the hole in our hearts.

Also remember this: if there is anything that will mess with your head, it is when you are so tired that you can't think straight. The Lord said that we need a day of rest. Don't make important decisions when you are tired. *Elijah was running on empty.* Have you ever been there? His mind was tired, exaggerating threats on his life, filling him with fear to the point that he wanted to die. He saw himself as a failure, but it all wasn't true. You are not a failure, and in Christ, you will never be one. Why is it that we can do so many great things for God or for our families and when someone says one negative thing, that is all we remember? *Elijah needed rest* and sleep to hear God's voice and to get his mind right. So do you. Sometimes we need to step away from the drama (the wind, the earthquake, and the fire) to get perspective. We need to sleep and go to the cave to hear God's still small voice. You need to minister to yourself before you can help others. It's not selfish; it's smart.

You know, every time I get on a plane they make an announcement before the flight. You are told if the oxygen mask comes down first, put it on yourself before helping your child. You have to take care of yourself first before you can help anyone else. This isn't about being selfish. This is about reality. Sometimes you are so busy worrying about or really enabling someone else that you destroy yourself and bring the family down with you. Enabling is just another way to not face the truth.

You see *the real problem is in the mind* and how we think about things and what we believe to be true. Am I going to listen to my emotions or deal with the truth?
Will I believe what God's word says?

So what is the answer? It is realizing that *not all our thoughts are true.* At times, we all think all sorts of unreal emotionally negative thoughts. We all think stupid things. *Emotions and feelings aren't always logical.* We can change our situations and our thinking. We can change our perspective. Life is not black and white or everything or nothing.

When we *overgeneralize* everything, it is either good, or nothing is good, and then we can begin to feel sorry for ourselves. When we begin to feel sorry for ourselves, we become the victims; we set ourselves up for failure. We blame everyone and everything around us. If there is anything that will destroy you, it is blame. By blaming, we become the victims, seeing ourselves as having no control over our own lives. You know, the poor-me attitude. Elijah thought that he could not win; he lost hope. This can lead to frustration and frustration to anger, and anger can lead to abuse of ourselves and others.

But my question is: Why would Elijah forget about God? Why would he lose faith? Why would he lose hope? I think Elijah became depressed. Depression can cloud your thinking about everything.

Maybe *Elijah felt depressed* because it seemed that every time he confronted Israel about their sin or even showed them God's power, *they rejected him.* They called him the "troubler of Israel." Even the widow that he lived with, for whom he performed miracles to feed her family, rejected him, saying, *"What have I to do with you O man of God? You have come to me to bring my iniquity to remembrance, and to put my son to death."*

When you're a Christian expect to be rejected; expect the world to not accept you because you remind them of their own judgment. By proclaiming Christ, you tell the world that there is someone, something, greater than self. John tells us that we are not of this world, and that is why they hate us. Jesus said that if they do this to me, what are they going to do to you? Elijah just could not accept one more rejection. He gave up; He lost hope.

In the *midst of the storm*, focus on His truth. *Focus on what you know.* God is real; seek Him. Jesus said, "I am the way, and the truth and the life..." (John 14:6). Jesus said, *"Come unto me all you who labor and are heavy burdened and*

I will give you rest...." If we build our lives on His truth, we can weather any storm. Remember that the boat can't sink as long as the storm or water stays on the outside. The real battle is what goes on within your head.

Above all, remember that no matter what happens in this life, *He loves you* and will help you through it, and He will use it for His purpose and glory.

In Luke 18, Jesus tells of the widow who would not give up seeking the judge for help. He tells us to ask, to seek, to knock, and we will find. The idea is: don't give up! Keep looking to God for the answer with relationships and situations. He will give the help.

2 Chronicles 15:7: "*But you be strong and do not give up, for your work will be rewarded.*"

And Elijah was rewarded. God remembered his faithfulness, and He will remember yours.

Look at verse 5b–6: "*All at once an angel touched him and said, 'Get up and eat.' He looked around, and there by his head was some bread baked over hot coals, and a jar of water. He ate and drank and then lay down again.*"

This proves beyond the shadow of a doubt that God is like an *Italian grandmother*—or at least my Italian grandmother—because one of the few expression I remember from her is, "*mangia, mangia*" (eat, eat). You know that real difference between the Italian part of me and my Jewish side? The Italians have better food.

When life seems unfair, when you have come to the end of your rope, and when you feel like giving up, God will send an angel. When life seems unfair and when you look for help, and it hasn't come, God will compensate you and bless you; He will send you your angel. The Bible says *that some have entertained angels unaware.* God, at one time in the past, just might have sent you a real angel, and you just didn't see it. God is an architect, and He is creating something for you and within you. Your angel might be a Bible verse, a book, a radio show, a friend, a counselor, the right medication, or even a song, but God will send you an angel. Is there *anyone here who God has blessed in spite of your circumstances, in spite of your pain*? Has God sent you your angel? Don't give up, stand firm, and wait on the Lord. God hasn't brought you this far to let you fail. Will you trust Him? Your angel is coming. God is building something in spite of your problem. He knows about your issues, and He cares, and He will help you through it.

I remember one of the lowest times in my life: when I thought that I was going to lose it all, and I got a *phone call* from my friend Pastor Ralph Didier, and it made all the difference in the world. It gave me hope; it restored my faith. It was a touch from the Lord. Do you need a touch from the Lord? Open your eyes, wake up, and see God's angel. He or she might be sitting next to you. Or *maybe you can be someone's angel.* You know that the word *angel* just means messenger. If you're struggling, God has a message for you today.

I don't know where you are at today; I don't know what you are struggling with. But God knows, and He has not forgotten you. I believe that He is cooking something better for you. He is bigger than any issue you face. I believe He wants to help you, and He will help you. You are right where you are supposed to be at this moment in your life. God foreknew; God knows all and understands all. He knew you from before the beginning of time. The question is: Will you seek His truth and His love? God has a purpose for your life and where you are at. You are a part of His plan, and He will work it out for His glory. No matter what you are going through or what you have gone through, God will use it for His glory. He has made you who you are—flaws and all—for His purpose.

ARE YOU LIVING LIFE OR IS LIFE LIVING YOU?

Through this struggle, *God was preparing Elijah* for Elisha. And even as Elisha was plowing in a field, God was preparing him to take the mantel (the ministry) of Elijah. What is God preparing you for? Elijah's future was to be greater than his past. Dear Christians, our future is greater than our past because our future is with God and for His glory. Funny fact: Elijah, the man who *wanted to die never did die*; God took him to heaven in a chariot of fire. Where is God calling or pushing you?

"If you keep doing what you are doing you will keep getting what you are getting." That is very true. If you keep doing what you are doing, where will you be in one year or five years? If you are not happy now, if you don't change things, you won't be happy then. Is the Lord challenging you to change your mind? Is He saying for to you to stop making excuses, to stop blaming others for your life? Is His Word speaking to your heart? His Word is hope. In the quite of this moment, God wants to heal your soul. Do you need *healing* within your spirit? He wants you to turn around your thoughts. He wants you to trust in Him. God is challenging you to change your mind. *There is nothing as powerful as a changed mind.*

When God closes a door, He opens a window. Can you *see the possibility* of having a better life? Do you have hope for the future? The Word will give you hope. His Spirit will give you power. Do you have a hope for a better life? Do you have a hope that your life can be better? Don't let life get the better of you. God wants and has more for you. This could be your moment to let Christ change your life. He wants to bless you; are you ready to receive it? Or have you lost your hope? I don't know about you or what you are going through, but I am not going to stop praising God for my life. *I am not going to stop blessing the Lord and hoping in Him.*

123

Chapter 7   Self Questions

1. How do you react when things don't go as you expect? Do you withdraw and get depressed? When did you start acting this way? Did something trigger your first disappointment?

2. How long does it take you to get over your disappointment?

3. List the things that you have lost because your reactions.

4. Is there a dream or a hope that you had that never came to pass? How does that make you feel to think about it?

5. Are you stuck in the way that you respond to problems and situations? Do you blame someone for your struggles? What is your part in the situation?

6. Can you see the possibility of having a better life? Why or why not? Is this logical?

7. Is there anyone you can trust to help you or give you advice?

8. If life feels so hopeless, how have you made it this far?

9. Are you running on empty? Do you make snap decisions even when you're tired and worn out? How might you get some rest? Is there any place that you can go to find rest and peace and direction for your life?

10. What do you think about this statement: "our feelings lie to us"? Could they be lying to you right now?

Chapter 7   Homework

1. If you are struggling with depression or disappointment, choose a half hour in your day to allow yourself to be as depressed or as upset as you wish. Use that time each day to express your frustrations. When the time is up, go back to being responsible and taking care of your business. Get up and force yourself to go to work and do what you need to do. Practice this for a week and evaluate if there is any progress.

2. Find someone to talk to or some group (like a church or service organization) to be a part of; listen to *uplifting* music or radio talk shows, or read things that provide direction.

3. Find a peaceful spot that you can go to.

4. If you are struggling with depression, check with your doctor to see if there might be a physical cause.

Chapter 8

FORGIVENESS

Ephesians 4:1ff

As a prisoner for the Lord, then, I urge you to live a life worthy of the calling you have received. Be completely humble and gentle; be patient, bearing with one another in love. Make every effort to keep the unity of the Spirit through the bond of peace.

Verses 26–27:
Be not angry and do not sin, do not let the sun go down upon on your anger, and do not give the devil an opportunity.

Verses 31–32
Let all bitterness and wrath and anger and clamor and slander be put away from you, along with all malice. And be kind to one another, tender hearted, forgiving each other, just as God in Christ also has forgiven you.

Here, Paul is writing from a jail cell. His life has been filled with turmoil. He has been whipped with 39thirty-nine strokes, five times, stoned three times, and turned on by his Jewish countrymen with death threats and assassination attempts. He has argued with the Apostle Peter over bringing the Gentiles into the church. He has been abandoned by his father in the faith and traveling companion, Barnabas, and now he is in jail, fighting for his life.

What blows my mind is that if anybody had a reason to be bitter or angry with God and with life, it would be Paul. He purposed in his heart to serve the Lord, and look what he got for it: trouble from the outside world and more trouble, even from the church. Was that what he signed up for? Can you relate? Have you been hurt by those you love? Do you lose your temper? But Paul was the real deal. The love of Christ lived in his heart. Paul was a radical Christian. Anger and bitterness didn't run his life. His eye was on the prize: the high call of Christ. His heart was pure, and God used him to bless and influence the whole world.

God blesses people that He can trust. Can God trust you to use what He gives you for His glory? Or are you selfish? Paul was blessed because, like the text, Paul was tenderhearted and forgiving, and he truly understood the forgiveness of Christ. God used him to change the church; God used him to change the world. He wrote the majority of the New Testament.

Do you say that you love God, but His peace is not in your life? Are you one of those people that goes from zero to ticked-off in a second? Are you one of those people that is controlled by anger, hurt, and bitterness? Are you one of those people who has a list of those, even in your own family, that you will never talk to again? All of us have had hurt, pain, and conflict in our lives. But, *we have a choice to let our hurts control us, or we can use our hurt to help others.*

If you call yourself a Christian, the last thing you should be is unforgiving and judgmental. Jesus commands us to love others, to be different from the rest of the world. If we couldn't do it, Jesus wouldn't command it. It was the love that Christians showed in the ancient world that set them apart. The true teaching of the church is that in Christ, in His forgiveness and love, there is no slave or free, rich or poor, male or female, Jew or Gentile—true equality. We are all sinners saved by grace. Do you have a problem loving others who don't look like you, believe like you, or agree with you?

The book of Hebrews warns us:

> *See to it that no one misses the grace of God (the free gift of love and forgiveness) and that no bitter root grows up to cause trouble and defile many.* —Hebrews 12:15

The real question is: How do you react when you are hurt or offended in life? If you think it won't happen, you are sadly mistaken. Is your heart so hurt that you are afraid to love or trust again? Can you trust that the Lord will deal with those who hurt you? Do you believe that people will reap what they sow? Do you have a hard time realizing that God's peace and joy are real? You might be smiling on the outside, but God looks at and judges your heart. Some of us have thoughts and hearts that are not pure; bitterness has taken root in us. It is the attitude of your heart that blocks your blessings.

Paul warns us in this chapter of Ephesians, as it says in verses 26 and 27: "*Be not angry and do not sin, do not let the sun go down upon on your anger, and do not give the devil an opportunity.*" Don't let the devil win.

The Gateway of Anger

It is okay to get angry. God gets angry; Jesus got angry. It can motivate us, but when we hold anger inside, over time it spoils us and begins to control us. It can cause us to misread, prejudge, and take every little slight personally. It takes control through our emotions, and we don't see it. We open the door for our enemy, the devil, to influence us, but more than that, it robs us of the presence of the Holy Spirit in our lives. Paul tells us in verse 30, Anger and bitterness can rob us of the joy and peace that God wants for us. It robs God's presence in our lives.

Does God's Spirit speak to your heart? Do you know that He is with you today? But how do you feel about loving others? Is it I love you, but—? I love if you look like me, act like me? Believe like me?

Beware: anger and unforgiveness can become an addiction. It is easier to be angry than to deal with our fear, hurt, or frustrations. I have heard it said, "Hurting people hurt people." *It is our struggles with others that are like a medication to deter us from facing our own pain.* I would say the real issue underneath the anger is the feeling of being unloved or rejected. These real issues are just too hard to talk about. It is easier to be angry and not have to feel. In that sense, anger is a drug.

There is a message behind the anger that is too painful to share. I remember my own mother's anger: after my father remarried, just the mention of his new wife's name would send her into a rage. The jealous rage was the feeling that she had been replaced, that all her years of struggling and loving my father meant nothing; in other words, she meant nothing. One gauge of how a person has forgiven another is when the old hurt is spoken about, does that person still become angry?

I would say that the more you can articulate your real feelings, the healthier you are. Yelling and showing anger come from when we feel weak inside. Anger is like beating your own drum. Again, it comes from the feeling of being a victim. Sadly, we tend to abuse or hurt others that we feel safe to abuse. Whether it is the destruction of property or picking on a little guy, anger comes from an attempt to overcome our own weakness and hurt. I would also have to say that controlling others with anger has an empowering effect for the aggressor; it feels good, which reinforces the negative behavior. In all that, it has an intoxicating effect! Therefore, you see that anger in many ways is a drug.

Dealing with anger is a lot like playing a sport: it is a skill that we can learn. We have a choice; we don't have to let it control us. We have the help of God's Spirit in our weaknesses. Paul tells us that love is not easily angered. Genesis 4 tells us that we must control it.

For real healing to take place, we need to dig out anger like we would dig out a splinter. We need to deal with the person or the situation that hurt us, *confront them or it,* and then give it over to God for healing to take place. Too often it seems that we react as if we have a splinter within our hearts. We don't want anyone to touch it, so we don't trust; we don't open up because we are afraid to get hurt again. Suddenly it seems that if someone gets too close, we push them away, all at the same time wanting to be loved and accepted. So we settle for relationships that don't get close, that don't touch the heart.

Do you have splinters in your life that God needs to heal? It is the attitude of your heart that blocks your blessings and that controls your life.

Have you ever been angry at someone, at life, or at God? I have. I had anger inside of me for many years: anger when I thought of my father. I thought that he never really loved me. I felt hurt. I didn't realize that he was doing the best that he knew how to do. He didn't know how to love himself, let alone me. He didn't know how to give or show me the love that I needed; he didn't know how to show it to anyone. I took responsibility for my father's anger and critical perfectionist spirit. I thought there was something wrong with me, or that I always messed up. I continued to beat myself up to try to please him until I got to the point of rebelling. I didn't understand that it wasn't all my fault. You can't please critical, angry people. People can't give you what they don't have. I just gave up on him and others in authority like him. Over the years, I have seen so many people take the anger that they have for a parent or toward someone who has hurt them and transfer it to everyone. It ends up spoiling their lives and hurts the lives of everyone around them.

The truth is that only God can fill the emptiness of our hearts and our need to be loved.

Therefore, Paul tells us from our text in verse 23, *"To be renewed within the spirit of your mind."*

Is it hard for you to admit your weakness or your hurts? Are you overwhelmed with life? Do you wonder where God is in your life? Can you bring your weakness and your anger to God? Can you open your heart to even pray for those who might have hurt you? If you're a Christian, God will give you the strength to do this.

Paul prays that we would understand life from God's perspective and love. In Ephesians 3:14–19, he tells us:

[14] For this reason I bow my knees to the Father of our Lord Jesus Christ,[a] [15] from whom the whole family in heaven and earth is named, [16] that He would grant you, according to the riches of His glory, to be strengthened with might through His Spirit in the inner man, [17] that Christ may dwell in your hearts through faith; that you, being rooted and grounded in love, [18] may be able to comprehend with all the saints what is the width and length and depth and height— [19] to know the love of Christ which passes knowledge; that you may be filled with all the fullness of God.

Paul saw the condition of our broken human hearts. He saw that the problem of our conflicts with one another was *really a spiritual problem*. He saw that without Christ, our minds and thoughts were confused and without hope. He prayed for revival, a revival in our hearts, a revival in our minds, and a revival in our soul. He prayed that we would understand just how much Christ truly loved us. He asked that we might comprehend, that we would understand the width, the depth, and the height of Christ's love for us—that Christ ultimately went to the cross that we might be changed, that we might be filled with His Spirit and be united with Him. Do you understand that love? Are you filled with His Spirit? Do you have His peace?

Real Forgiveness

Forgiveness and real healing begin with the right relationship with God. It is knowing that all your sins are forgiven: past, present, and future. It's realizing how much Christ did for you personally on the cross. It is understanding the debt that you have been forgiven. It's in knowing the depth of His love for you.

Paul says in our text,

> *"Be kind to one another, tender hearted, forgiving each other, just as God in Christ has forgiven you" (v. 32).*

Have you ever loved someone more than you have loved yourself? Maybe your child or spouse? That's how much Christ loved you in that He emptied, He humbled, Himself, even to the point of death on a cross for you. It's a love that transcends life and death.

Have you ever loved someone, even though they have died? Do you even love them more since they have gone? It's a love that is stronger than death itself. Can you say today that you know that depth of love? Do you know in your heart and in your soul how much Christ loves you and has forgiven you? If you were to hear the words "it is cancer," would you trust that all things work for the good, and that even if you were to die, you would be with the Lord? Paul, knowing that his life was on the line in jail, could say that to die was gain. Could you? It's knowing that in the midst of the storm that you're not alone. With that kind of love, there is power over life and death.

But I have a question: If you know how loved and forgiven you are, then why do some of you have such a hard time forgiving others? Do you think that you can live the Christian life and harbor unforgiveness in your heart? The enemy wants to steal your power, your hope, your love, and your witness. Do you really believe that if you stop loving, stop caring, or if you don't forgive that you will be able to protect your heart from being hurt? That's a lie! The only thing you do is cut yourself off from those that you say you love. You just end up hurting yourself and those close to you. If you hang on to bitterness and unforgiveness, it would be better if a millstone were hung around your neck and you were thrown into the depth of the sea.

Jesus tells in His great prayer to forgive us our debts, trespasses, or sins as we forgive those who sin against us. He goes on to say, "For if you forgive men their transgressions, your heavenly Father will also forgive you." So what does this all mean?

Doesn't this verse say that I am praying for God to treat me like I treat those who have hurt me? Are we praying, "God forgive me as I forgive others"? But doesn't it also imply that we are praying, "God curse me if I curse others"? "Judge me as I judge others"? Don't let your unforgiveness rob your blessings, rob your joy, or rob your peace. Forgiveness is something that you do for yourself. It doesn't mean that you accept that what was done to you was right or that you pretend that it didn't happen. Forgiveness means freedom for your heart and your soul.

It is freedom from the burden of keeping a record of all the wrongs done to you. Real forgiveness is in apprehending God's love and forgiveness and letting it overflow to others. The question really is: Does your behavior match your faith? Jesus said that you will know true believers by their fruit, i.e., their actions. Do you lose it when things don't go your way? Do you keep a record of every wrong done to you? Paul said that you can say all the right things and believe all the right things, but if you don't have love, all your sacrifice means nothing.

How do you deal with conflict? What do you do when someone hurts your feeling or offends you? In Matthew18, Jesus tells us to go to that person, one on one, and then with a witness, and then within the church, and if they don't listen, *let them go; let it go.* Just those words could be a message. If you understand "let it go," you have learned enough. Here are some rules that have helped me in dealing with people and confrontation:

- **"Put your cards on the table.** Share your feelings. You say things like, "When you do this or that it, it really hurts," or "I feel hurt; I wish next time you would please…," but if they don't want to do something about it, if they don't want to *ante up* or try to change, that isn't your fault. If they are not willing to listen to how their behavior continues to hurt and try to change that hurtful behavior, it is not unfair to tell them truth. Paul again in Ephesians 4:15 tells us, *"To speak the truth in love."* In that way we grow up to what God called us to be. He goes on in verse 25 and says, *"Laying aside falsehood speak truth each one of you to his neighbor for we are members of one another."* If people don't listen or react to your truth, it is okay to let them go or not let them be an intimate part of your life. The problem many times is that then we feel rejected and try harder to get them to accept us, but they just don't care or know how to. That isn't your fault.

- **Don't rescue or enable.** Remember that the father let the prodigal son find out the hard way. We need to let people be responsible for their actions. I am reminded of one mother who, for years, gave and bailed out her son for every responsibility in life. He never learned how to think for himself and be self-sufficient. He only learned to manipulate her and others to get his needs met. Over time, he still wanted her money, but in the end, he despised her. These two people became stuck in a sick relationship where both lost.

- **Don't take things personally.** If a person treats you in an unloving way, odds are that they treat everyone that way. It is not just you! There is a saying, "If it don't apply, let it fly." If a person says things to you that you know are true, don't worry. Our problem is that we tend to focus on the negative.

- **Understand that everyone is doing the best they know how.** The craziest behavior makes sense to the person doing it. Jesus said, "Forgive them for they know not what they are doing" (Luke 23:34).

- **Admit your mistakes.** The Bible says, *"Confess your sins to one another and pray for one another that you may be healed" (James 5:16).* It is hard to admit when we were wrong, or that the way we see things hurts us and the people that we say we love. Not only this, but it is equally as hard to go back and make things right with the people we have hurt. My suggestion is that when you're wrong, when you have messed up, admit it *quickly.* People see it already, and they will respect your honesty. Take responsibility and pray with and for the people you have hurt. Beyond this the next step is *to make it right* with the people that we have harmed, to ask for forgiveness, and to restore the relationship. This is a sign of real maturity.

- **Mourn the loss.** Many times you might not get the results that you hoped for, but then it is time to mourn the loss of the relationship and move on. Jesus said that there is a time to *"shake the dust off your feet"* and move on. It is almost harder to mourn the hope of the relationship and the dream for that relationship that you had in your head. It is not that the divorce is so bad (it is; I am not advocating divorce), but it is the loss of the dream that you had in your head for that relationship that is harder to accept. You had this idea of how your life would work out, but things or dreams were not going according to plan. Dealing with that loss is sometimes the hardest. The idea is to not let that loss stop you but to move forward and to not let bitterness grow inside you.

- **Forgiveness doesn't mean trust.** It doesn't mean forgive and forget. The Bible still says that we reap what we sow. If a spouse cheats and asks forgiveness, does that mean that we accept him or her back right away and act as if nothing has happened? That would be foolish. Just because that murderer says that he or she is sorry and asks for forgiveness, the murderer still goes to jail. People need to earn trust; they need to show that they have dealt with their issues before we open our lives to them. An important skill in life is to know whom to trust. It is differentiating who really cares for you and who doesn't or doesn't know how to. It's knowing who's got your back, and who doesn't.

- **Get love where it can be found**. You can't go to a critical, angry person and expect to find love and acceptance. Jesus said, *"A bad tree cannot produce good fruit" (Matthew 7:18). "Don't give what's holy to dogs, don't cast your pearls before swine [meaning angry, critical, judgmental people],…they will turn and tear you to pieces" (Matthew 7:6).* If a person doesn't care or love others or even himself or herself, how will he or she ever love you? You can't go to a critical, angry person and expect to find love and acceptance.

- **Watch the feet.** Actions speak louder than words. It's not what people say, it is what they do that counts. Learn to listen, even with your eyes, and accept the truth of your relationships. If people tell me that they love me but their actions tell a different story, I accept that and move on. Jesus said, *"You will know them by their fruit" (Matthew 7:20). Fruit,* to the Hebrew mind, means actions.

What does faith have to do with forgiveness and confrontation? It is realizing that the battle belongs to the Lord. It's realizing God that is in control. It's knowing that God can and will use the situation for your blessing and His glory. With the understanding that God is in control, it gives you the ability to have *an attitude of reconciliation and forgiveness.* It's all about attitude. It's about trusting God. It is our faith that is the victory. It is realizing and trusting, *"No weapon formed against me shall prosper" (Isaiah 54:17).* In fact, it is our faith that overcomes the world.

Jesus said, *"If your eye [your attitude] causes you to stumble pluck it out…."* Jesus is saying that if you look at others with an attitude of pride, self-righteousness, greed, lust, and hate, get rid of it. These are the things that send us to hell. It is our attitude that separates us from God and others. It is the attitude of your heart that blocks your blessing. Jesus makes the point again in Matthew 18:21–22 when He tells Peter that we must be willing to forgive a brother who hurts us seventy times seven times, meaning, really, an infinite number of times. We need an attitude of willingness to forgive. We need to forgive because in love Christ forgave us. By the way, because I had a willingness to forgive, I was able to lead my father, the Jewish atheist, to Christ a few months before he died.

The Bible says again in Matthew 18 that when two people forgive each other on earth, they will be forgiven in heaven. When two people come together in His name, in His power, in forgiveness, Christ is in the midst. The verse, *"Where two or more are gathered in my name…," is really in the context of forgiveness.* Christ's presence is in forgiveness. There is a spiritual reality and component to forgiveness. When we forgive and when we are forgiven, He is here. When we forgive one another, I feel that there is rejoicing in heaven.

The Bible says that we grieve the Holy Spirit; we lose the presence of God when we hold on to anger and withhold forgiveness. We open the door for Satan to influence and destroy our lives. We fall for the snare of the fowler, the enemy. In fact, with unforgiveness, you are giving power over your life to the person that hurt you.

Jesus said that if you are giving an offering to God and remember that someone has something against you, make it right first. Otherwise, the enemy will destroy you. Jesus says that you will end up in the jailhouse. How many people are in prisons of their own making? It's your choice.

Dear friend, God looked down from heaven and saw all our hurt, all our suffering, and all our conflict. He saw our lost condition; He saw our sin, our hopelessness, and He said, "I love you; I love you; I love you." God became man. That's who Jesus was. He was God. He made the blind to see and the lame to walk; He fed the five thousand because He cared for us. He brought us into a new relationship with His father by dying on the cross and taught us the real meaning of forgiveness. Have ever felt that forgiveness? Let God release you from your bitterness and anger. His forgiveness is the gift you give yourself. It costs too much the hold on to the hurt. It leads to self-abuse with drugs, food, isolation, and the loss of joy and peace. Forgiveness is so important that Jesus prayed for our forgiveness from the cross.

We have forgiveness because Jesus Christ, the Son of God, went to the cross. The blood of Christ called out forgiveness to God the Father. It calls out that you can't hide your sin, your hate, and your bitterness. His blood, His life, brings everything to the light. What is the truth about you?

Christ gave His blood, His life, to forgive you. Are you washed in the blood? Do you really have that relationship with Christ? Or are you faking it to make it? There's a smile on your face, but underneath, do you harbor anger, bitterness, or fear. There is power in Christ's forgiveness and reconciliation. It is the victory; it is the only real forgiveness. Through the cross, Christ takes away the power of the enemy, the power of bitterness, and hate. Through His forgiveness on that cross He overcame the powers of sin, and He conquered death. He gives you the power over sin and death as well. When we choose to forgive, we get power back in our lives as well.

I remember watching the *Tonight Show.* Jay Leno had a special guest on named Louis Zamperini. He was ninety-five years old. He had been in the 1936 Olympics when he was nineteen years old and had shaken hands with Adolf Hitler. During the war, he was shot down in the Pacific and survived on a raft for forty-seven days (still a record; when rescued, he only weighed sixty-seven pounds), only to be placed in a Japanese POW camp. There he was beaten repeatedly, tortured, and scheduled for beheading. Because of his fame as a runner, they tried to get him to do propaganda on the radio with Tokyo Rose. They flew him to Tokyo, but he refused to go on the air. He was then beaten and tortured again. After the war, he returned home to marry his sweetheart. But the horror that he went through caused him to have nightmares of torture every evening. He began to drink in order to run from the memories. It got so bad that his wife was filing for divorce, but she went to hear Billy Graham, where she gave her life to Christ. She returned to Louis and told him that she wasn't leaving due to the fact that she had become a Christian. But she said, "Louis, you need to go hear Billy Graham." He did, but he still would not accept Christ. But he came home and began to think to himself, saying, when he was going through all that hurt, all the horror, he remembered how he promised to serve God if He got him through it. He said to himself, "God kept his part of the bargain; now I needed to keep mine." (It really was a miracle that he survived all that he had been through.) The next day he went to the crusade and accepted Christ. The funny thing is that from that night on, the nightmares stopped. He eventually went back to Japan and personally forgave the guards that hurt him. That might be the first and last time I heard the gospel on the *Tonight Show.* There is real power in the forgiveness of Christ. It is the presence of Christ that changes our hearts and minds.

The Bible teaches that anger, bitterness, and unforgiveness rob us of God's peace and presence in our lives. But when you give your life to Christ, the separation is removed; the heart is changed from one of stone to one of flesh— a heart that can love and forgive. The hate and blame that used to control you no longer bother you. When you think of the past, it no longer brings up bitter emotions. That's how you know that Christ has healed you. When you come to Christ, He will heal your heart and make it tender again so the Holy Spirit can use it in Christian living.

Maybe you're saying to yourself, "I have been hurt so much, why should I trust anyone or even God again?" Do you know the sin that sends more people to hell than any other? The greatest thing that stops us from accepting God's forgiveness and forgiving others is pride. Pride keeps more people out of the kingdom than any other sin. It was the devil's sin. It was the original sin. It was the sin that was first committed. It was the sin of selfishness and pride, and God hates it. Pride will keep you from coming to Christ.

Are you too proud to ask for forgiveness? Are you too proud to forgive someone in your life?

Are you at the point of losing your marriage, family, children because of unforgiveness? Your battles are within your home, at work, with those around you, and most of all with God. The problem is in how you think about things and people. Anger and bitterness are destroying your life. How long do you think you can play this game?

The Bible says, *"How can we escape if we neglect so great a salvation?"* (Hebrews 2:3). How can we disregard the blood of Christ? So many lives are run by spite, hurt, and revenge. As long as you continue to be unforgiving, you are going to have conflict and hurt. You are going to have a war within your own soul. You are going to have troubles, conflicts, and problems until you come to the cross and seek the forgiveness of Christ. Until you drop your pride and admit that you need God's forgiveness, you will never truly understand or be able to forgive. The Bible says, *"He that loves not knows not God for God is love"* (1 John 4:8).

If God, the Holy Spirit, is speaking to you, if there is unforgiveness in your heart, you had better come to Christ, or you will be in danger of hardening your heart. That is dangerous. It would have been better for you not to read have this book than to have read it and go away and do nothing about it because you put another ring of hardness around your soul and heart.

The Bible tells us in Psalm 44:21 that God knows our secrets, our hurts, and our hates. In Jeremiah 17:10, the Bible says, *"I the Lord search the heart."* The Bible teaches that we cannot hide anything from Him. He knows all our secrets. It is out in the open before Him right now.

Proverbs 21:2: *"Every way of a man is right in his own eyes."* Do you need God's forgiveness? Do you to need to seek forgiveness from someone you have hurt? Jesus said, *"If you forgive others their sins your heavenly father will forgive you" (Matthew 6:14).* Is the Holy Spirit speaking to your heart right now?

Is there a little voice down inside of you right now, speaking? That is the voice of the Holy Spirit. He is warning you. He is rebuking you. He is pointing His finger at you. He is making some of you uncomfortable. It is God, the Holy Spirit, preparing your heart to be forgiven or calling you to forgive someone today.

Jesus said, *"Come to me all you who labor and are heavy burdened, and I will give you rest" (Matthew 11:28).* He will give you peace. He will give you forgiveness.

Let me tell you about a friend of mine named Gloria (not her real name). I met Gloria when she was fourteen years old, and she was filled with bitterness and anger. She could be happy one moment and break into tears the next. Even though she had grown up in a rough neighborhood and members of her family were in gangs, she wanted to be a good schoolgirl. At age eleven, that all changed. While walking home from school, a group of gang members raped her. In order to cope with what happened to her, she joined her brother's gang and began using drugs. She began carrying guns and doing the things that gang members do. One night while partying, drunk, and on drugs, she was holding a gun, and it went off, killing her brother. She shared this as we sat in a counseling group together. Every time she mentioned her brother's name, she would break down and cry. Her family disowned her. They could not forgive her, even though it was an accident. They also took no responsibility for letting the drugs, guns, and gang in their home. Gloria ultimately turned to God for forgiveness. Most of all, with Christ's help, she was able to forgive herself. One day in our group, she announced that she had decided to become a nurse and help people. Eventually, she moved home and then out on her own because her family still wanted nothing to do with her. She has now graduated high school and is looking forward to nursing school. She still keeps in touch and visits our groups to tell her story and help others turn away from their negative lifestyles.

I am humbled by her and by God's forgiveness in her life. God makes clear in His Word that if you are to come into the kingdom, if you are to be forgiven, you must come by faith and receive Christ.

When you come to Christ and accept and understand His forgiveness, you receive a new heart. The Bible teaches that old things are passed away, and that all things have become new (see 2 Corinthians 5:17). You enter into a new way of living. You enter into a new life. Life has a new purpose, a new meaning. There are still problems and hurt, but peace and joy reign in the midst of them. Let Jesus come in and accept His forgiveness. He can do it right now. Maybe you need to be forgiven? Maybe you need to forgive someone else. Maybe even yourself?

If you want Christ, just pray,

Dear Lord Jesus, thank you for dying on the cross for me. I know I have done wrong and I ask for forgiveness. Fill me with your Spirit and help me to change my life. Right now I want to live my life for you. I give up living for myself, help me. In your name I pray. Amen.

Chapter 8   Self Questions

1. What is the worst thing that you have ever done to someone else?

2. Without hurting that person, can you ask him or her for forgiveness?

3. Is there a list of people that you need to seek forgiveness from?

4. Who would be on top on that list?

5. What are you doing in your life to deal with yourself so you don't continue hurting these people?

6. Are you avoiding asking for forgiveness? Why or why not?

7. How have your actions affected the lives of those you have hurt?

8. Is there a time when you can begin to make things better? Are you committed to this?

9. Do you ever feel guilty? How do you deal with the feelings of guilt in your life?

Chapter 6   Homework

Set a time to seek and ask forgiveness from the people that you can.

If it is someone who has died, write a letter asking forgiveness and then burn it.

Chapter 9

LOVING LIFE

The greatest question of life is: Why am I here? What was I created for? Do you really know who you are and what you have been given? Why would God bring you this far in your life? Is it for nothing? There is a purpose for your life. If you're His child, He has a plan and a future for you.

Do you know what God wants for you?

Micah 6:7–8: "He has shown you, O man, what is good; and what does the Lord require of you but to do justly to love mercy and the walk humbly with your God."

How can you enjoy and rightly live the life that you have been given?

What really makes life good? God created the world and said that it was "good." He created man and woman and said that it was "very good." Happiness is realizing that we were created for a purpose: to reflect God's glory and ultimate goodness. As Jesus said, real goodness is only found in God. It's knowing that God created you, and that He gave you your abilities; He has gifted you to deal with life and to serve others. It's in knowing that you are wondrously made for His glory. You were created to praise Him. Psalm 150:6

tells us, *"Let everything that has breath praise the Lord."* You were created to have a relationship with the living God. Do you really know Him?

Do you know what the good life really is? It's realizing that He is the reason that you exist. You were created for His glory and by His grace. It's realizing that if not for His grace and mercy, you couldn't have come this far. It's realizing that if not for His love, you would not have made it in this life. It's knowing that He loved you more than He loved himself; He died for you.

That's why when life happens—when the hard times come. I don't give up. I know His love will never fail me. He will never leave me or forsake me. He lifted me out of the miry clay; He placed my feet upon the rock. I love Him more today than yesterday—because I know that He holds me up when I am down. He gives me hope. I have lost friends; I have lost family; I have lost things; but He is still here. Even if life gets rough and I have to face things that are uncomfortable, when I hurt, I know that He will help me. He helps even if I don't always feel His presence. Sometimes we go through the hurt—out of love, He gets us on our knees to bring us closer to Him. *"Faithful are the wounds of a friend."* He loves us enough to lead us to and show us the truth. He might even close doors in our lives to move to where we need to be. I know that He did this in my life.

If you don't know this, then you don't know what happiness is; you don't know what real faith is. Are you honest with yourself about your life and your relationships?

Micah tells us to do justice and to love mercy. Do what is right toward ourselves, others, and God. Have an attitude of mercy and love! Do you treat others fairly and rightly? Do you know that in helping others, in loving others, you help yourself and honor God?

Now you might be saying to yourself, "I really don't love and trust people; I would rather be alone than risk possibly getting hurt." God said, *"It is not good for the man to be alone."* God created us for relationships.

Real isolation drives people crazy. I am not suggesting that we have deep relationships with everyone we meet. One trick in life is learning who truly cares for you and who doesn't. The trick is avoiding those who are only out for themselves.

But life is about seeing how God has blessed you and believing that He will bless you as you bless others. We need to get involved in serving others if we want to take real steps toward a fulfilled life. God has called you to be a priest—to have a ministry in helping others. Real life—real joy—is showing God's love and mercy to others.

Being a Christian isn't about following a bunch of rules. It is not about "thou shalt not," but it's about "thou shalt love." It's about loving God and sharing that love. As His priest, you are called to give your body as a living sacrifice and to praise Him with your life and service for others. When you focus on helping and loving others, you find real peace and power. There is power in the unity of believers and in ministry; in this purpose, there is joy. It starts by just giving a hand to someone in need. The problem is that so many take "love" to only be a feeling. But love is an action. Feelings change with the wind, but love is eternal and powerful within itself.

If we wish to overcome our past hurts, it helps to help others who are hurting as well. In helping others, we no longer become the victim. We become empowered through our service. I have spent the last thirty-plus years serving the Lord and helping others. I have been the one who has been blessed.

How can we live and walk humbly with our God in the midst of this crazy world? How can we walk in His presence when things go wrong or when things don't go as we plan? How can we know and show His forgiveness throughout the trials of life?

Perspective, Thankfulness, and Praise

Too often we take things in this life for granted. Somehow, we think that tomorrow is promised, but it is not. God is in control of this life; it's His life—His gift. God is going to do His thing in your life. You are called to trust Him in spite of circumstances and to know that in spite of everything, He wants to—and will—bless you. It's when your expectations of life get in the way of reality that you have problems.

The Jews teach us in the Passover that "life is dipped in tears," but it is still a gift, and we have the choice of what to do with it or how to think about it.

There once was a godly woman who, in one day, lost her two sons in an accident. In the stress of the situation, she wasn't sure how she would tell her husband of the tragedy, because he loved his sons so much. When her husband returned home, she shared this story: "Many years ago a man gave me two beautiful jewels to hold for him. Today he called and asked for them back. What should I do?" she asked.

The husband replied, "Of course give them back."

Then she took him to the room where the bodies of her two sons lay and said, "These are the two jewels."

Perspective is everything. It can change your past and guide your future. We don't have God's perspective or know how He will work things out for our good, but He will, He promised us who believe that He knows our future; He knows eternity, and we don't. He has promised us a future. He has a purpose for our lives and will use everything, even the hurts and pain of our lives, for His glory. Remember what Jesus said to Martha concerning her brother's death? "If you believe, you will see the glory of God." If you believe and trust Him, you too will see God's glory.

My wife and I went to Nepal. In preparation for the trip, my missionary friend Saji told me that I would be teaching a group of about forty pastors and evangelists. But he didn't give me any real ideas about what they needed, He said, "Whatever the Lord puts on your heart—just be uplifting." I didn't how many hours I was supposed to teach. All I knew that it was to be three days. Some of those who came traveled eighteen hours on a bus just to be a part of the conference. I had to speak through a translator, but many of them spoke English and even had seminary degrees. What could I tell them? I kept on praying and seeking what God would have me to say.

Two nights before it was to begin, in a dream I found myself asking, "What do I need to teach?" And I heard a voice say, *"I will bless the Lord at all times; His praise shall be continually in my mouth."* I woke up about four in the morning with those words running through my head. The problem was that I didn't know what verse it was or where it came from in the Bible. So I did what anyone would do: I did a Google search on my phone. It is amazing when you think about it—I was on the other side of the world in the middle of who knows where. We had seen Mount Everest flying in, and I was trying to find a verse on Google. Sure enough, it was Psalm 34:1, word for word. From that, my teaching and, unexpectedly, my counseling fell right into place. God gave me the right words for the right time.

I've concluded that it is a choice to praise God and bless Him when all hell is breaking loose in your life. It is a choice to worship and trust God when your bills are piling up, and the doctor says its cancer, or you a get that phone call in the middle of the night, and a voice says that your son has been in an accident. It is a choice to praise and trust God when the world around you looks like it is going to hell in a hand basket. It is in the understanding that God is God, that God is still on the throne, and that He still loves you. The world and hell itself can't comprehend it when we trust and worship God in spite of the harsh realities of life. *"Though He slay me, yet will I trust Him"* (Job13:15). Do you really believe that *"all things work together for the good for those who love God and are called according to his purpose" (Romans 8:28)?* God has a purpose for you and for what is going on in your life.

It is the understanding that worship is what we were created for. *"Let everything that has breath, praise the Lord" (Psalm 150:6).* There is joy in that truth. It is in the understanding that we will be praising at the throne of God for all eternity, and it will be as one moment. As the last verse of "Amazing Grace" reminds us: "When we've been there ten thousand years, bright shining as the sun, we've no less days to sing God's *praise* then when we first begun." We will be praising Him for all eternity.

God has blessed me; God has blessed *you;* He has blessed us with life. He has blessed us in the *past,* and He will bless us in the *future.* He died on a cross because He loves us. He has set us free from sin and death. He has given us new life. Remember, *"It is no longer I who live but Christ who lives in me...and the life I live now...I live* by faith" *(Galatians 2:20).* Know this: our life doesn't belong to us; it belongs to God. My wife, my kids, everything belongs to God. Our life is a gift of His grace; He can do with it what He wills. As Job said, *"The Lord gives and the Lord takes away, blessed be the name of the Lord."* Will you choose to trust and praise Him? *"Faith is the substance of things hoped for the evidence of things not seen...without faith it is impossible to please Him"* (Hebrews 11:1ff). *"This is the victory that has overcome the world, even our faith" (1 John 5:4).* It is our faith in Christ alone that gives the victory; it is Christ who gives us hope. Is Christ what you hope for? It is about faith in Him and the cross and not ourselves.

It saddens me that our society is so obsessed with *self.* The "I am going to get mine" philosophy is prevalent from individuals to megacorporations. It's not that money is evil; it gives you more options. But it is not to be the love of your life. Seek Him, and He will give you what you need. If you truly want to enjoy the life you have been given, it begins in the realization that *it's not all about you.*

We need to be thankful for each day that we have been given. We need to *realize* that it isn't all about us or about self. Selfishness and self-centeredness is the root of all sin. All of us really want control, but it isn't about us; it's about Christ. We must choose to trust Him. Each day has His divine purpose within itself. It isn't that easy to do, but through that understanding, we can have peace.

Philippians 4:4ff says,

Rejoice in the Lord always; again I say rejoice. Let your forbearing [patient] spirit be known to all men. The Lord is near!

Be anxious for nothing, but in everything by prayer and supplication with thanksgiving, *let your requests be known to God and the peace of God which surpasses all understanding, will guard your hearts and minds in Christ Jesus.*

Giving thanks each day can change your mind-set throughout the day; in fact, the verse says that it will guard you. It will protect you from things like bitterness and frustration. There is joy in just being thankful that you are alive. It is in being thankful for your relationships with God and others that you can gain a different perspective on life. It is realizing that He will never leave you or forsake you. Do you look to His living word to gain truth and insight? That has the power to change us and to help us look at things in a different way. From gratitude comes real peace; it will protect your heart.

Real Happiness

Where can we find this elusive thing called happiness? Is it in buying the bigger house, in the nicer car, or in hoping that in the purchase we will find satisfaction? Some people go from one relationship to the next, hoping that in that they will find true happiness. Others use one substance or another to try to find that thing that will make life better, but emptiness always returns.

Proverbs 17:22 says, *"A cheerful heart is good medicine, but a crushed spirit dries up the bones."*

The truth is that people with an unhappy spirit, people who are caught in bitterness and anger can destroy their own health and relationships with everyone around them. Too often people are overcome with bitterness, jealousy, and hate. Do you know that God can and will help you to deal with the hurts of life? God still heals a broken heart. I have seen Him do it. In contrast, a person with a thankful heart, a cheerful heart, a happy optimistic spirit makes all the difference in the world. Happy people can refresh the spirits of everyone around them. We need laughter; we need joy. A pastor friend told me many years ago that you need to laugh a lot in life because most times you just feel like crying. Happiness and a good sense of humor seem to counterbalance the negatives of life—physically and spiritually.

What kind of person are you? Are you really happy? I don't know about you, but it's the happy people that make the world a better place. It's the happy people that make a difference in this world. Not only do they make everyone around them feel better, but as this verse tells us, it is good for their own soul and body. Happiness helps them in the healing process. There seems to be some medical evidence to back this up. According to one recent study, happy, optimistic people even live longer. When you know God loves you, when you know He has your back, you don't need the world's or others' approval. When you focus on the things you have lost or on those who have left you or who didn't love you, you can lose your joy and forget to give thanks.

Faith and Relationships

So where can we truly find happiness, real happiness? Jesus, in the Sermon on the Mount, said,

> "Blessed are the poor in spirit for theirs is the kingdom of heaven. Blessed are those who mourn for they shall be comforted. Blessed are the meek for they shall inherit the earth. Blessed are those who hunger and thirst for righteousness for they shall be filled. Blessed are the merciful for they shall obtain mercy. Blessed are the pure in heart for they shall see God. Blessed are the peacemakers for they shall be called sons of God."

Over and over in this text Jesus uses the word *blessed*, but what does that really mean? The word itself comes from the Hebrew word *barakh*, meaning to kneel, to bless, and to praise. It is related to how you feed a camel. To feed the camel, you need to get it on its knees. I guess, in a sense, that is also true for people. To be fed or blessed by God, you first must get on your knees. *Barakh* can be also translated *happy*. It is really saying that happy are the people whose spirit is humbled or meek before God. The Bible says that the beginning of wisdom is fear (meaning respect) of the Lord (Proverbs 1:7a). Ultimately, as I look at this text, Jesus is saying that real happiness comes from a right attitude, a pure heart (right motives), and the right relationship with God. This is what Micah means by walking humbly with our God.

The problem for many of us is that we want control of our lives. We are afraid to trust God or others. We want the world to revolve around us, but it just doesn't. So we grab, and we strive to make things go our way without putting God first, and we lose this thing called happiness. Happiness is hungering and thirsting for the relationship that we need with God. Jesus says, "Blessed are the peacemakers." The thought is: happy are the people who've made their peace with God. My point is that I am not, you are not, and we will never be happy, as long as we look for the happiness or peace within ourselves or in things.

True happiness is found in our relationship with God and in the relationships of family and friends. It is in the bonds that we make. It seems that we live in a world where relationships are put aside. We're so busy running and working to get things—the things that we think will make us happy. Because of this striving, we miss out on the thing that truly does make us happy, which is relationships. It seems that many have traded real relationships with other people for obsessions with Twitter and Facebook, where many people write "look at me; look what I am doing; look what I have done." Do you spend your life working for things and position? Do you need to tell the cyber world every move you make?

Do you live your life looking and working for the approval of others? When you know that God loves you, when you know that He has your back, you don't need the world's or others' approval. When you focus on the things you have lost or on who has left you or didn't love you, you can lose your joy and forget to give thanks.

Freedom

The greatest power in all creation is a changed mind. It is knowing God's will for your life and having the freedom and power to live out that truth. It gives you the ability to overcome past hurt, fears, and jealousies. It's knowing that God is with you in your struggles, and He will help you through life.

God gives us the power to deal with life. He gives us the power to freely choose, to grow, to trust Him, and to live a life that glorifies Him. It's our free choice.

Happiness is about faith and the freedom to choose. We need the freedom to make mistakes to grow, to change, and to trust God and His power to deal with life. We need to be free to pursue happiness. We need to be free to be able to make the decisions that open the doors for our lives. Freedom gives us the opportunities to live the life God called us to. *There are many today who believe that the government should provide all their needs. That government should control their lives for their own protection.* Happiness isn't found where the state or government takes care of us. That type of thinking leads to dependence, and dependence leads to anger and hopelessness. God gives us the freedom to choose Him. He lets us use our minds and live out our hopes and dreams as we walk by faith. Being coddled and taken care of really doesn't bring happiness; it brings misery and slavery.

It is in the ability to work, to strive, and to accomplish things for God's glory that we truly find happiness. It is when we feel that we have no choice and no options for the future where hopelessness, depression, and bitterness take over. It is in the freedom to make the choices and work things out that we find real happiness. That's why communism or fascism never work.

It's in the working out of problems, in accomplishing and looking back and saying to yourself, "job well done" or realizing that it was by the grace of God that you made it. How many couples don't look back at the years when they were struggling and made sacrifices to start a family and say that it was the best time of their lives?

Faith

If you are looking for this thing called happiness, realize that lasting happiness isn't found in things or in fleeting pleasure. Real happiness is having the presence and reality of God in your life. It is something that happens within your heart, your mind, and your soul.

Ultimately, true happiness comes from faith, not just faith in self or in self-esteem but from faith in God and living for a higher purpose. It has to do with loving others and ultimately loving God more than you love yourself. Many people have never loved anyone or anything more than themselves. All their past hurts and fears get in the way.

Have you ever really given yourself to God? It might mean walking away from your old life, letting go of old hurts, letting go of revenge, bitterness, relationships, or even philosophies. It is saying, "God I love you more than all of these things." That is the sacrifice that God wants and honors. This is what it means to walk humbly with your God. What have you let go of for God? What have you had to trust God for? To get something new, you have to let go of something old: old values, an old life, old struggles, or maybe even old dreams. Jesus said, "Come to me. I will give you peace." But to come, you must leave past bigotries, hurts, and fears. It is realizing what Christ sacrificed for you. He left His glory in heaven and became a man for the greater glory of saving your soul.

> But we all…beholding as in a mirror the glory of the Lord, are being transformed into the same image from glory to glory, just as by the Spirit of the Lord. —2 Corinthians 3:18

When you realize this is when you will see a real miracle in your life. You will realize that you are the miracle.

Then you can say, like the apostle Paul, "I have learned the secret of having abundance and suffering need [contentment]. I can do all things through Him who strengthens me" (Philippians 4:12b–13). Faith makes all the difference in the world. The Bible says that it gives you the peace that passes all understanding. It's also realizing that it's not all on you; it's in knowing that there's a God who loves and cares about you personally, and you will never be alone. More than anything else, this truth, this revelation, will give you the peace and happiness that you strive for. Do you know that peace today? You can, by asking Christ into your life today.

It is as simple as praying, *"Dear Jesus, I give up. I will do whatever you want me to do; help me,"* and then trusting Him for the outcome. You just do it! You commit your life to Him and do your best to obey and follow His leading, shown to you in the Bible. As Mary, his mother, said to the servants at the wedding at Cana of Galilee, *"Whatever he says to you, do it."* In the doing, you will find real happiness. Jesus said, *"Seek first the kingdom of God (loving God and serving others) and all these things (ultimately happiness) will be given to you"* (Matthew6:33).

How it all worked for me:

Before I confronted my life, as I said, I spent much of my time running from life, running from myself, and running from my self-imposed situations. I generally didn't like people telling me what to do, even though underneath I think I really wanted direction, guidance, and ultimately love. I had a problem trusting, wanting so much to be able to trust. Like so many people, I was running but not knowing where I was going—let alone knowing how to get there. Maybe you have felt that way as well!

Through my use of drugs, I feigned happiness. The only problem was that I could not build relationships with others. I had friends—or you might say, acquaintances—but generally, things were superficial. The other major issue was that I could not hold a job. I was in and out of employment and different colleges, trying to pull things together but not finding that niche for myself. I remember one morning waking up in my step van in which I lived and saying to myself after a night of partying: *I don't want this anymore.* Within a few weeks, I sold the van and found a place to live. This was only the beginning of my journey. I still found myself not dealing with my depression and escapism. I just blamed the system and the world around me for my unhappiness.

Although not a real choice of my own, I was asked to attend a church by a young lady. Not because of any spiritual awakening but actually for purely carnal selfish reasons, I decided to attend. To be honest, church was something truly foreign to me, having been raised in a Jewish home. In fact, I was proud of being Jewish—at least intellectually or culturally. I saw myself as an agnostic. I believed in God through my Jewish upbringing and with experimentation with LSD, but I lived life as a virtual atheist. I had a natural dislike for Christianity, having been told in Hebrew school that Hitler was a "good Christian." I remember thinking how hypocritical Christians were. I believed "Onward Christian Soldiers" was about killing Jews. Still, a pretty face can outweigh bigotry.

Relationships come and go, and with only selfish motives, this one, like others, evaporated before my eyes. I thought that maybe this time things would be better, but I was confronted with another self-directed failure. Thinking as a true victim, I thought that I could never win, no matter how hard I tried. (I am sure this is a negative thought from my childhood.)

So with the great powers of my intellect and my best thinking, I decided to commit suicide on Christmas day, 1977. Actually, this made sense, since escapism and withdrawal had been a pattern of my life for many years. In my deluded thinking, I believed that I would be making a statement to God and the world by choosing Christmas day. Like Jacob in the Bible, I think I was wrestling with God (or at least subconsciously with my father).

You might call this crazy, but God is good!

A few weeks before Christmas, I had a dream: I was in a beautiful green mountain valley. I felt love and peace, and I heard the voices of what I guessed to be angels, singing (a cappella) the most beautiful music I had ever heard, in seemingly infinite overlapping harmonies. I remember telling myself in the dream, "I wish I had a tape recorder." Then as I stood there, I saw a bright radiating light in the distance, and as it got closer I realized that it was Jesus. It was as though the light was penetrating through me, and I felt love. I didn't want the dream to end, but suddenly clouds came, and it began to rain and thunder, and everything changed, and I felt pain. With that, I awoke around three o'clock in the morning, thinking to myself how strange this dream was. I fell back asleep, and when I got up again, strangely the words of the twenty-third Psalm were running through my head. I remember that the last phrase was especially vivid: *"Surely goodness and mercy will follow me all the days of my life, and I will dwell in the house of the Lord forever."* Oddly, I had never really read the Bible before, but I must have seen those words.

Honestly, I just thought it was a dream. Days went by, and I still struggled with my depression. I made the connection to pick up some heroin and began giving my things away, even my truck. I knew that I really didn't want to die, so I went to the free clinic at my college. I told the doctor how I was feeling, so he gave me a prescription, and I told him that I didn't want to be on medication. I knew that I had been self-medicating for years, and that didn't work. So the next weekend, I went to see an old friend. He was a counselor whom I respected. We sat in his apartment, talking and smoking a joint. For some reason in our discussion I asked, "Is there a God that loves and cares about you?" That's what I had been told, I said, when I would go to this little church, and it made me feel good. He told me that it was nothing; we make ourselves feel good. That seemed to make sense to me. Then he told me to see what really makes you happy—what's real!

The next day was Sunday, and I was determined to see if God was real. I woke up early, so I decided to walk to this little church. It was a few miles, so I spent time talking to God, looking at the animals along the way. I remember saying, "If you made this, it was gorgeous," but I still doubted, remembering how I was told, "We make ourselves feel good." As I sat thinking these things, clouds suddenly came in, and it began to rain and thunder. I said to myself, "That's a coincidence; it's like that dream I had two weeks ago, but God can't be real; it's all in my head." Then someone rang the bell for the service to start.

So I got up, and a man handed me the bulletin for the service. On the front were the words of the twenty-third Psalm: "The Lord is my Shepherd…." At that moment, I felt God tugging at my heart. I said to Him, "I give up; whatever you want, I will do." God must have a sense of humor: after that service, a woman came up to me and said, "You play the piano; we need someone to play for the choir tonight." I have played in churches ever since.

Within the next few weeks, I had read the Bible, and I celebrated Christmas for the first time. As I continued to read, I began to feel convicted about my drug use. By the end of January, I prayed that God would take those cravings and thoughts away, and He did. I have never gone back to drug use. Not that I am perfect or some spiritual giant. I still have to face life and learn to be responsible for who I am and what I do. It has been through my relationship with the church and family that I have grown toward maturity. Most of all, it has been my relationship with the Lord and the knowledge of His love that has kept me strong. It has given me the ability to love the life that God has given me and to live it for His glory. I have learned not to self-medicate, but for a while I switched addictions for food rather than drugs and still get obsessed at times with work or music. But now they don't control me; now I have the joy of living life rather than life living me.

I guess the last question is this: Have you given your life to Christ? Are you sure of it? Have you had an encounter with the living God? Do you know Christ personally? Do you know that your sins have been forgiven? If He came back today, would you be ready? If you had one day to live, would you have peace? Have you surrendered your heart?

Chapter 9   Self Questions

1. Do you love your life? Why or why not?

2. What do you think about the statement, "In helping others, you help yourself"?

3. Is there anyone or any group that you would want to get involved with or help? Do It.

4. What issues or persons do you need to confront to move on with your life?

5. Make a list of the things or persons that you are thankful for.

6. Examine your relationship with God. Does it help your life? Why or why not? What do you need to change to make it better?

Homework Chapter 9

Memorize and live these "**LIFE PRINCIPLES.**"

1. **PUT GOD FIRST.** Realize that life isn't all about you. You were created by God for His purpose and glory, not yours. Life is God's gift, so be thankful and enjoy it. Get your priorities right and trust in the Lord, and peace will follow. Share His joy with others.

2. **IN HELPING OTHERS, YOU HELP YOURSELF.** Life is a place to support one another, so focus on solving "here and now" problems. Personal character and spiritual growth reveals itself in daily conduct and through interaction with others.

3. **HONESTY** (to yourself, others, and God) **IS MOST IMPORTANT.** Keep it real.   Note: That doesn't mean that you say rude or angry things to others that you know will hurt them.

4. **IF IT DON'T APPLY, LET IT FLY.** Don't take hurtful comments *personally.* There are reasons and real reasons why people say and do what they do. Many times it has nothing to do with you. If you know that it's not true, ignore it. But accept all feedback—good or bad—and evaluate if there is something you need to change.

5. **GET LOVE WHERE IT CAN BE FOUND.** A person cannot give you what they don't have. An angry, self-destructive person, who can't love himself or herself, can't love you the way that you need to be loved. Don't ignore red flags. These people are not safe; *stay out of their way.*

6. **DON'T JUSTIFY** or make excuses for poor behavior. Take responsibility for your actions. When you are wrong, admit it. Don't take responsibility for other people's (children's, parents', friends') issues. It doesn't help. Let them learn that there are natural consequences; otherwise, you reinforce poor behavior. Let others fall or be responsible for their actions. Show them the way back up. Deal with your own issues first. *The only person you can change is you.*

7. **REALIZE PEOPLE ARE DOING THE BEST THEY KNOW HOW.** The craziest behavior *makes sense to that person.* We are all human. No matter how hard we try to live a good life, in the end, we all make mistakes; we all have faults that we don't see. In light of this, we need to model openness, honesty, forgiveness, and understanding. Real leadership is the influence we have in reflecting God's love to others.

8. **RESPECT EACH OTHER.** Every person has worth given them by God. In respecting them, we respect God and His gift of life.

9. **LISTEN, LISTEN, LISTEN.** Pay close attention to what those around you are saying and how they are acting. *Watch the feet.* It is not just what people say, it is what they do. Listen with your eyes as well as your ears. Right action follows right listening.

10. Use **"I STATEMENTS"** in resolving conflicts with others. Keep your sharing focused on your feelings. Say things like, "I feel…when you…. Next time, could you please…?" Life is not a place for name calling or put-downs. Losing your temper is a sign of weakness.

CLOSING THOUGHTS

There are many things that I don't know about life. I don't know why I had to bury a six-year-old child who died of cancer. I don't know why a wife and mother dies, leaving a husband and two children. I have traveled to many places in this world and have experienced and heard stories of suffering, murder, and abuse. But I do know this: *life happens.* All of us have faced and will face tragedy and pain. There is no way we can escape it. The question is: Will we let the painful situations of life control and destroy us, or will we use them to grow and help others? In the Western world, we seem to think that we can control, legislate, or buy our way out of every tough situation. That is a lie. We falsely believe that life revolves around us, but life isn't about us; it's about God. The truth is, life is not fair, but God is.

God has made you who you are and has given you the grace to deal with your life. Your life is not some mistake. He has given you the power to live life abundantly. Jesus said, "Peace I give unto you not as the world gives." But you need to give your whole self to Him. You need to trust Him with all your heart, mind, soul, and strength.

We can never know the answers to all the whys in this life, God's ways are not our ways, and we are not His counselor. So focus on His truth. *Focus on what you know.* God is real, so seek Him. Jesus said, *"I am the way, and the truth and the life…" (John 14:6).* If we build our lives on His truth, we can weather any storm. *"But they that wait upon the Lord shall renew their strength;*

they shall mount up with wings as eagles, they shall run and not be weary; and they shall walk and not faint" (Isaiah 40:31). Again David says, *"I will bless the Lord at all times His praise will be continually on my lips" (Psalm 34:1).* There is power, joy, and peace in trusting God. It's your choice. Respect, love, and praise Him. As much as you can, enjoy the life that He has given you and share it with others. Above all, remember this: no matter what happens in this life, *He loves you* and will help you through it, and He will use it for His purpose and glory.

For I am persuaded that neither death nor life, nor angels nor principalities nor powers, nor things present nor things to come, nor height nor depth, nor any other created thing, shall be able to separate us from the love of God which is in Christ Jesus our Lord. —Romans 8:38–39

Made in the USA
Columbia, SC
23 October 2020